TRICKS AND MORTAR

TRICKS AND MORTAR

The Little Book of Property Wisdom

Laura Henderson

Book Guild Publishing
Sussex, England

First published in Great Britain in 2011 by
The Book Guild Ltd
Pavilion View
19 New Road
Brighton, BN1 1UF

Typesetting in Garamond by
Keyboard Services, Luton, Bedfordshire

Printed in Great Britain by
CPI Antony Rowe

A catalogue record for this book is available from
The British Library

ISBN 978 1 84624 541 1

Contents

Introduction

Homeownership in the UK has been a dominant force in UK society over many decades, providing comfort and stability to millions of families, and giving life to the labour-intensive construction sector. Yet by idealising the investment upsides, many of us have ignored the downsides at our peril. The credit-crunch inspired recession has seen the resulting fallout, with house price falls, repossession increases and a negative equity epidemic that could take years to eliminate.

For most of us, however, buying a home still remains the preferred, and indeed, the smart choice. On paper, putting almost all of your liquid assets into bricks and mortar may seem foolhardy, but in practice it often works out beautifully, with the loan paid off ahead of retirement, a mortgage-free pad in which to spend your golden years, and a valuable and tradable asset to pass down the generations.

The consensus among industry pundits is that cult of homeownership will continue – the allure of home-sweet-homedom now so embedded in our collective psyche, that its growth is guaranteed. That doesn't mean, that we shouldn't continue to question the virtues of buying, nor ignore the trade-offs involved in tying ourselves to an illiquid investment. Owning a home is not for everyone, but if you're willing and able to assume the responsibilities, the tools of the trade to pursue your dream are within your reach. In fact they're just over the page . . .

Laura Henderson

1

Boom and Bust

1 It's only supply and demand

'I am like any other man. All I do is supply a demand.'

Al Capone

There's no secret or conspiracy to it: property prices ultimately fluctuate because of the interplay between supply and demand. Why? Because the ebbs and flows of local residential tides come at points when a market runs out of purchasers willing to pay a higher whack or when buyers get frozen out by restricted funding – mortgage availability being a key culprit. When demand cools, price rises are certain to reverse, stopping the market in its tracks. The fundamentals of supply and demand are the foundation on which all markets are built, and while supply tends to change in discrete chunks as new houses or estates become available, demand ebbs and flows according to sentiment and confidence.

Bottom line: All things being equal, when demand exceeds supply, prices will rise.

2 Keep a clear head

'Look at market fluctuations as your friend rather than your enemy; profit from folly rather than participate in it.'

Warren Buffett (US businessman/investor)

Bulls (glass half full investors) and bears (glass half empty investors) can both make money in a variable market. It's those who get caught up in the moment and overreach themselves who usually come unstuck. A core characteristic of the 'bandwagon effect' is that it's self-fulfilling – when investors see the price of property falling, the herd mentality takes over, and many run for the hills, which in turn fuels further falls. Experienced players, on the other hand, stay focused on the fundamentals. They stick close to the property pack but remain on the fringes. This way, they don't get trapped in the middle of the panic when the next stampede comes. So, don't let immediate market conditions and short-term shocks mess with your head. Property troughs are normal and are not a reason to sell quality at a loss. Always have a Plan B in your back pocket for moments when the market picks up, which given time, it always will.

Bottom line: Keep a clear head and pick a long-term strategy.

3 Choose wisely

'Buy land, they're not making it anymore.'

Mark Twain

When seasoned investors believe the market is entering a down phase, they switch to buying up property in the best areas they can afford, as they know that these neighbourhoods usually boom again early on in the next cycle. Why? Because demand seeks the highest affordable supply quality. Adopting this approach means they can leverage their investment by selling on earlier in the upturn and buying elsewhere. More importantly, they remain one step ahead of the property pack.

Investment in up-and-coming areas is often driven by inflation in adjacent popular patches. These areas, too, will pick up momentum and eventually peak as they are swept along with the tide of the boom cycle, but they won't peak first, so buyers will generally have to wait longer to see any returns. Savvy investors work to enter such areas as the affordable supply in adjacent areas dries up. They then tend to sell up just before the heat goes out of that market, enabling them to once more buy the most they can afford in the best possible area and thereby position themselves for the next cycle.

Bottom line: In a downturn, buy in the best location you can afford and look for 'wannabe' neighbourhoods once the recovery gains momentum.

4 Get your timing almost right

'The way to make money is to buy when blood is running in the streets.'

John D. Rockefeller

Picture the scene. A leather-clad Tom Jones is belting out his final number at the O2 and you reluctantly call time on your trip down memory lane and make for the nearest exit. Those extra few minutes put you ahead of the crowds and home in time to catch the last of *Newsnight.* Better to have sacrificed the finale, than been stuck for hours in car park chaos, even if it meant missing out on the 'It's Not Unusual' swansong.

Timing your real estate move can and should be viewed from a similar 80/20 perspective. Sometimes you need to forgo even the strong likelihood of a significant immediate return for the probability of a smooth expected transition to the next investment.

Broadly speaking, early in a slump is the time to keep an eye out for 'forced' sales, particularly of the new-build variety. If the economy does take a sustained dive and as job losses start to show in their usual lagged fashion, it's newer owners who are often forced to make a hurried sale. In the middle of a slump, it's the cheaper neighbourhoods that begin to feel the pinch and bargains as well as distressed sales begin to appear. Towards the end of the down cycle is the time to bag luxury property bargains and potential renovation projects in sought-after neighbourhoods. The well heeled take that little bit longer to feel the pain.

Bottom line: Timing is everything. Don't run to the crowd's timetable – make your own.

5 Down doesn't have to mean out

'The best time to buy a home is always five years ago.'

Ray Brown (author)

Low levels of buying interest suggest a property cycle has finally done its dash. At times like these, people often expect the market to drift along in the doldrums forever. So, not a good time to be buying, you might think, with confidence so low? Wrong. A house bought in the down cycle might not provide the same 'drip-feed' guarantee of a steadily appreciating price tag. But what prospective buyers do have going for them at the market nadir is the rare luxury of a wide choice at an affordable price. Compare that to the boom times when decent purchases are snapped up before they even hit the market, with a surfeit of buyers chasing the limited stock of 'ideal' homes. So how do you go about bagging a 'downturn' bargain?

Establish a fair market value – research the most recent selling prices of comparable homes in your chosen area; not the asking prices, but the offers that were finally accepted. Local agents and in-the-know neighbours can be tapped for this kind of information.

Tweak your offer terms – think about what negotiation nuggets you have to offer that will sweeten the deal in your favour. Most vendors will, for example, be amenable to a price cut if they know there's no chain, you're able to move quickly and can provide supporting evidence of comparable 'under-value' sales in the area.

Launch a charm offensive – the first few weeks of a new listing are critical, particularly if there are other potential buyers in the frame. So keep the lines of communication open with both the agent and the vendor; provided you can deliver quickly, certainty, speed and a healthy dose of courtesy are often enough of an incentive to secure the deal.

Bottom line: When the property chips are down, there's always a trade-off between price and flexibility.

6 Sell high but be realistic

'Wine is valued by its price, not its flavour.'

Anthony Trollope

We've seen a seismic shift from the days when 'testing the market' with a ceiling-breaking price tag was a one-way bet to wealth. Adopt a strategy like this in a downturn and your property will be left languishing on agency books. Why? Because in a buyer's market, the 'usual' value indicators – what you originally paid for the place, how much you've shelled out on renovations, even how much profit you need to make – carry little sway. Top of the billing, instead, is what the buyer can afford and what they think they can get away with offering.

So how do you secure a fair outcome without giving your house away? As bizarre as it may sound, pricing *below* the competition can ultimately put you, the vendor, back in the driving seat. By undercutting the market, and asking for 90 per cent of the perceived value, your house will look like a 'bargain' compared to your neighbours. You're also much more likely to achieve your asking price, as buyers will be shopping around for properties where sellers have already priced in incentives.

Bottom line: Your house is only worth what someone is willing to pay for it.

7 Look for clues

'It's better to look ahead and prepare, than look back and regret.'

Jackie Joyner-Kersee (US athlete)

It's a seductive prospect: catching the wave of an early property boom before it becomes fashionable. Buy a place, sit back and watch your capital value rise. So what green shoots should you be looking out for? What are the tell-tale signs that the good times may be about to roll again?

Long-distance links – upswings generally show where the downturn first took hold. In today's globally connected economic climate, all eyes are on the US market to transmit the buy–sell smoke signals to the rest of the world.

Stabilising unemployment – more people in work means increased confidence, demand for properties and fewer repossessions. Bear in mind, however, that a reduction in unemployment always lags behind economic well-being. So, by the time unemployment reverses, the economy will have been growing steadily for several quarters.

Evidence-based research – The Land Registry, Acadametrics, and mortgage lenders including Halifax and Nationwide, offer comprehensive, user-friendly market reports, which can be accessed online. Check data specifically relating to mortgage approvals, price fluctuations, number of sales concluded and buyers registering interest.

Local motion – the absence of estate agents' boards, fewer new house listings and a dearth of property ads in the local paper, are clues that the market is bottoming out and preparing to climb back up. To check property price movements in your neighbourhood, review favourite listings on a weekly basis on *www.rightmove.co.uk* and *www.zoopla.co.uk*. If sales are picking up, it's time to get back in the game.

Bottom line: During times of change you need to believe what you see, not see what you believe.

8 Keep it real

'I always like to look on the optimistic side of life, but I'm realistic enough to know that life is a complex matter.'

Walt Disney

There's no rational reason to expect property to always be a sound investment. As with shares, it's the starting point that matters most. Shares have proven something of a disappointment over the past decade – over-promising and under-delivering. It has taken ten years for a combination of earnings growth and price falls to bring them back into line. A similar process has unfolded with residential property, a salutary lesson being the buy-to-let binge, which has left us with a post-recession glut of unwanted new-builds cluttering up the market. The illusion of 'housing wealth' has also prevented many of us from noticing that we've been struggling to maintain our standard of living, as real incomes have stagnated over the past 30 years. Given that the housing market rarely spends any time at 'the average', your house will always be either over or under performing the market at any given moment, so don't get too hung up about it. In the end, you're looking to get the best mix of financial and domestic outcomes from your property choice.

If there's one thing we can be certain of, it's another boom–bust cycle. Perhaps next time around we can look further ahead and hatch a smarter plan – recalibrate our expectations to more realistic levels: save more, value what we already have and spend more time and money on productive investments with long-term value. Our houses are, first and foremost, homes, places where our lives are lived, and in the end, our years of family fun will massively outweigh any financial leg-ups we may achieve along the way.

Bottom line: The property market is full of false beliefs – don't get sucked in.

2

Buy Right

1 Study the property seasons

'No winter lasts for ever and no spring skips its turn.'

Hal Borland (US author/journalist)

Any house purchase, no matter how small, should take account of the property seasons. Broadly speaking, the market picks up in early March and ticks over steadily before winding down in November in the run up to Xmas. While the end of the year brings a natural lull in the property purchase calendar, it's also the perfect time to grab some one-to-one attention from agents, as clients tend to be thinner on the ground. Play your cards right and you'll also get advance warning of properties coming onto the market in the spring, giving you the chance to get first crack at them.

Different buyer groups have their schedules too. For example, families with young kids often prefer moving during the summer holidays, so they've time to settle in before term starts. If your heart is set on something with

13

multiple bedrooms, this means getting your act together early in the new year. Couples and single vendors are a little harder to pin down, although research indicates that couples often move in the early autumn after a break in the sun.

Developers are equally susceptible to offers at key points in the year with most looking to boost their sales figures in the run-up to their financial year-end. To stand the best chance of a price reduction, aim to get your offer in four to six weeks before their end of year; company websites routinely log this sort of information. For limited companies, similar information is available through Companies House *www.companieshouse.gov.uk.*

Bottom line: Get to grips with the property seasons – knowing your 'highs' from your 'lows' can put you in the right place at the right time.

2 Separate the soon-to-be hip locales from the wannabes

'Profitability doesn't happen when you're walking on bullshit.'

Jerry Martin (American actor)

New cars, skips outside private homes and 'under offer' signs on retail premises are all tell-tale signs of a neighbourhood that's destined for better things. But real regeneration takes between five and ten years, maybe more – so it's important to look beyond surface changes. The property industry uses the term 'up-and-coming' as a cure for all ills, when it's often just sales person speak for talking up a down-at-heel area into some imaginary future gold-mine. To pass the soon-to-be hip test, any aspiring area worth its salt needs to deliver on a number of levels:

Property price growth – be wary of investing somewhere with a stellar track record; it could mean the neighbourhood has already reached the peak of its price potential. Your profit margins will be healthier if you plump for an area experiencing average growth. Not only will property be more affordable,(making your initial financial outlay lower), there's also the prospect of decent capital appreciation if you choose wisely.

Transport trends – more than ever in a developing district, the ease of getting in and out is crucial, so make sure that funding has been ring-fenced for transport improvements as opposed to 'in the planning stages'.

Homely highlights – put on some comfy walking shoes and check out what the neighbourhood has going for it in terms of commercial and recreational assets; coffee shops, a posh deli or bakery, and a sprinkling of estate agents all suggest a neighbourhood that's going places. But how is it managing its congested streets during rush hour? Is there ample space for parking and what's on offer for the area's 'yoof' of an evening?

Forward features – don't fancy moving in to discover a chippy is about to open at the bottom of your road? Enquiries at the local council will reveal if there are plans to redevelop a town or district. To be doubly sure, check planning applications with the help of 'Plansearch Plus' via the Landmark Information Group (*www.homecheck.co.uk*) or pay a small fee to your solicitor.

Bottom line: Don't be someone else's guinea pig – make sure your chosen district has something going for it already before you take the plunge.

3 Beware of white elephants

'There ought to be a room in every house to swear in.'

Mark Twain

Property location is key, but the architectural style and layout of a house also have a huge bearing on current value and future resale potential, so make sure you view all potential homes with a critical eye and always get a second opinion from someone you trust.

- **Don't** get distracted by 'bling' bathrooms and fancy fixtures and fittings or you'll end up paying over the odds; too many homes boast these extras, but fail to deliver where it counts – on plot size, proximity to services and natural assets like mature gardens and off-road parking.

- **Do** size up the living space – a house filled with lots of cosy, little rooms may look quaint, but it could be incredibly limiting compared to one with a smaller overall square footage and open-plan areas built in. Uneven proportions – one big bedroom and one box room – can be equally problematic, especially if you're planning to rent; tenants looking for two-bed properties will want decent sized bedrooms, not swing-a-cat shoeboxes.

- **Don't** buy the swankiest house in the street. It will enhance the value of nearby less expensive properties, but 'the best' has nowhere to go.

And a word of warning: if it's a bargain 'doer-upper' to let you're after, remember you'll have a mortgage to pay while you renovate before you can even start drawing a rental income.

Bottom line: Broad appeal sells best – always buy a property that's going to sell well when you decide to move on.

4 Think global – act local

'Don't buy the house, buy the neighbourhood.'

Russian proverb

Scan the newspaper headlines and you could be forgiven for believing that there's only one enormous property market that goes up or down. Instead, it's local indicators – a shortage of property, a strong local labour market and good schools – that ultimately influence what you buy, when you buy and what you end up paying. In a downturn, many local economies might actually still be expanding, but depending on the number of buyers and sellers of flats or resale properties, prices in these areas could be rising or falling – at the same time.

National property price surveys can be a useful tool for assessing overall upward or downward price trends as well as giving you an indication of how long it might take to buy a place, but they have their limitations. Some only cover mortgaged properties and omit those that might be sold and owned outright. This can lower the average property price quoted (as against other surveys) and give a skewed reading. Results can also vary hugely depending on what stage in the property sale process the market is 'measured'.

To get a true reading of a particular neighbourhood, turn detective: study local buy-sell rates, property trends, developments and demographics; your regional authority can provide up-to-date stats and facts on all of the above, as can websites such as *www.homecheck.co.uk* and *www.upmystreet.com.*

Bottom line: A little knowledge is a dangerous thing – be thorough with your research.

5 Bag a bargain

'It's just as unpleasant to get more than you bargain for as to get less.'

George Bernard Shaw

Riding the peaks and troughs of the market is always tricky, but when word on the street is that it's a buyer's market, it's time to listen up. If buyers can purchase without overreaching themselves and are willing to accept that their asset may dip in value, the slump represents an opportunity to grab a home at a knock-down price. Even so, it's still vital to target areas and properties that will be resilient, offer scope for improvement and will appeal to other buyers.

Bargain hunting basics:

Estate agents will always try and get the best price they can for a property, but their business relies on signed and sealed deals, so they'll be eager to shift homes that have been languishing on their books.

Try to distinguish between homes whose prices are reduced due to market conditions and those with genuine structural/location issues. Be thorough when questioning the selling agent and do your due diligence.

In the case of new-build, developers are invariably under pressure to sell to meet their own financing needs, so don't just accept the list price – always try for a lower offer.

Previously sold plots can be a good buy – these come

on the market when a buyer purchases a property off-plan (before completion) and has then been unable to complete the transaction. In most instances, the developer will have kept the original deposit and will be looking to sell the plot quickly, so you stand a good chance of getting the deposit amount lopped off the price.

Always dissect the discount – 30% off, is all well and good, but if the original price already has a generous mark up, the discount is more 'apparent' than real.

Bottom line: A bargain is only ever relative to true market value – and market value is a movable feast.

6 Be quick off the mark

'Savvy buyers are predatory about real estate. When they sense a softening, they move in for the kill.'

Andrew Cooper (real estate consultant)

Cash buyers are king in the property world. They have the 'readies' at the ready. If it's a pristine house in a prime location, chances are there'll be an oven-ready buyer or two waiting in the wings, even when the market's flat. Even if you've already exchanged on your own property, you'll still come a poor second to someone who's got the dosh sitting in the bank. So get prepped – have your deposit money ready and waiting and any mortgage approval signed off. Have a friendly surveyor on side, too, to magic away any 'spanner in the works' queries; and a lawyer with good contacts at the local authority.

Bottom line: Adopt the Scout motto when buying and 'be prepared'.

7 Know the difference between cost and value

'Price is what you pay – value is what you get.'

Warren Buffett

There's no fail-safe method of assessing the value of a property – an appraisal is an art form as much as it is a science. That said, a buyer should always have a ready-made 'formula' for determining a property's right price (from their perspective) and whether the investment is likely to be a profitable one. The following methods *when combined* work well:

The **comparable approach** focuses on factual market data of sales of similar property in a recent time period and gives an estimate of which price is adequate for a certain kind of property. Sales comparisons can be easily done using Internet databases of property transactions such as *www.zoopla.co.uk* and *www.upmystreet.com* and also through the Land Registry. The advantage of this method is that it reflects actual market prices, but it neglects the issue of whether a property investment is profitable for the buyer.

The **income approach** concentrates on the profitability of an investment and analyses the present worth of property on the grounds of its anticipated future resale value. In doing so, it gives a good appraisal of whether a certain property is worth its current price to the buyer. Three aspects need to be taken into account with this approach: the buyer's 'capability', the property's 'capability' and the buyer's future plans.

A buyer's individual capabilities reflect the resources they can bring to bear on the property. These include his or her time, knowledge, money and/or commitment. The less a buyer has of each, the lower the offer should be.

A property's capability is all about its income generation potential – this could be through rentals, tax deductions, grants for renovation, as well as the property's long-term appreciation potential; the ultimate goal being to sell at a higher price per square foot than originally purchased.

A buyer's plans for the property also have a bearing on its value. Does the house come with planning permission to extend, the option of acquiring additional adjoining land or converting outbuildings? Any plan that builds a property's potential value makes it more viable for the buyer to offer a higher price.

Combining these two approaches is the surest way of getting a true gauge of a property's value in relation to its asking price. As a buyer, you can subsequently determine the intensity of your interest in a purchase and set an offering price that makes sense. It's not hard to do, but most of us simply don't bother.

Bottom line: Don't make the mistake of equating cost with value – they are not one and the same.

8 Haggle like a pro

'Information is a negotiator's best weapon.'

Victor Kiam

Good negotiation skills pay dividends in the property world. If you're able to back up your argument with cold, hard facts you'll be in a much stronger position. Being able to refer to 'work needed' in the valuation report so you can wangle a price reduction, or pointing out that the asking price has dropped since it initially went on the market, gives a clear signal that you've done your homework. But the work doesn't stop there – effective haggling is all about leveraging information.

Once you've found your dream home and are ready to negotiate, allow the vendor to make the first move on price so you can gauge how much room for manoeuvre you have. As a general rule, an opening gambit of 10 per cent to 15 per cent below the asking price is reasonable unless you know for sure there are several offers in the bag. Back up this lower offer by listing what work you'd need to do on the property and what it would cost you. Above all, stay courteous and don't crowd the vendor. Estate agents tend to take a buyer's measured approach as a sign of serious intent – a cool-headed investor = a reliable punter.

Bottom line: Properties don't come with fixed price tags so get haggling; remember, the seller is probably being equally tough with whomever they're buying from.

3

Pundits and Players

'I climb mountains for the same reason an estate agent sells houses – to earn a living.'

Ranulph Fiennes (explorer)

1 Sort the agency men from the boys

It's easy to spot successful agents – they're the ones who've put in the time on their patch and have an instinctive understanding of the market. So how do you select the one that's best for you when selling a property? Personal recommendations may seem like a safe punt, but they should never take precedence over matching your property with the right agent. Your needs, budget and house spec may bear scant resemblance to those of your parents or your best friend – so why pick a firm to represent you that doesn't live and breathe your target market?

Any half decent agent shouldn't have to start cold when taking on a property. Get them to demonstrate similar houses to yours they've sold in the past twelve months, and explain where they found the buyers, how long they took to sell the properties and what prices they went for. Track record is the *only* way of measuring their performance – a good sales negotiator will not only be able to rustle up three clients with a ready budget of £200,000, but will also be able to identify the outsider prepared to offer £225,000.

Bottom line: There's only one way to pick the best agent – find the one with the track record in your price bracket.

2 Surf the online property playground

'The Internet is like a giant jellyfish. You can't step on it. You can't go round it. You've got to get through it.'

John Evans (media mogul)

Property portals with searchable databases of homes for sale now run into the hundreds in the UK, not to mention upwards of 18,000 estate agent offices with their own websites. Having that knowledge at your fingertips is a dream come true for property anoraks; but for the rest of us, looking to purchase a property, the only sure-fire way to get results is to streamline your search.

- Don't waste time and energy surfing small sites with low traffic – go where the largest number of people are buying and selling, which means the four major property portals – *www.rightmove.co.uk*, *www.zoopla.co.uk*, *www.findaproperty.com* and *www.primelocation.com*. Familiarise yourself with them all – each has slightly different audiences and regional strengths in terms of property volumes and price brackets.

- Always register your details on your favourite sites – you'll get e-mail alerts as new properties appear and 'catch' a house as soon as it comes on the market.

- New instructions (new properties for sale) tend to

29

be uploaded on estate agent websites overnight, so if you're looking for a house in a sought-after area, get online before 'opening hours'.

- Make the most of website content – if a particular property appeals, look beyond the basic spec; study the photographs and floor plans posted and take an interactive tour. If it's an area that takes your fancy, streamline your options and narrow your search to particular streets or a specific postcode.

- Many portals don't allow you to click through to the estate agent's website. To get round this, simply copy and paste the estate agent's name into Google. It saves time filling in tedious online forms.

- E-mailing estate agents can be a hit and miss affair with many not even bothering to respond. It's annoying, but if a particular firm has your dream property listed then bite the bullet and chase them up. Drop hints, such as 'ready to move quickly' and 'chain-free' and you'll galvanise even the most complacent into action.

- Don't rely on national surveys as a barometer of the local market. For a more in-depth valuation of properties in your target area, start at *www.hometrack.co.uk*. If a home has changed hands since 2000, you can find out the exact price paid for it, for a small fee, at *www.landreg.gov.uk* and *www.myhouseprice.com*. You'll also discover which property types are in most demand; you may, for example, be living in an area where there's a shortage of family homes, which could give you the leverage you need to up your asking price if you are selling a property.

- Few information sources allow homebuyers to take the temperature of the market like real estate blogs, and Twitter is top of the pile. The site can help you to follow the top agents in your area and stay on top of market changes, gossip and local news, as well as tap into a whole new group of contacts who are searching and dishing out local and national real estate information.

Bottom line: Quality, not quantity, is key to online research – so learn to discriminate.

3 Don't cut corners on conveyancing

'A great fortune depends on luck, a small one on diligence.'

Chinese proverb

Conveyancing is a competitive business, with a mind-boggling choice of solicitors, licensed conveyancers and online products now filling out the market. As options go, you could do a lot worse than plump for one of the larger established firms in your area. You'll pay a bit extra, but they'll be staffed up, have a 'live' network of authority contacts, work to service level agreements with agents and brokers, and deploy the technology necessary to move things through quickly. You'll also be able to tap into their expertise on specialist areas such as restrictive covenants, boundary disputes and planning permission, something you won't get with a 'fixed-fee' online service manned from a call centre in the back of beyond. E-conveyancing has its place in the market, processing one-stop transactions, but the impersonal 'conveyor belt' working style can be inflexible and grind to a halt if your case is anything but straightforward. Small high-street firms carry their own health warnings too. If they are understaffed and overworked, you run the risk of being stuck at the bottom of the 'to do' pile with the likelihood that the vendor will lose faith in you as a serious buyer and pull out of the deal.

Bottom line: Conveyancing is key – so go for the best you can afford, unless it's a simple, tick-box purchase.

4 Get on first name terms with the planners

'There are no rules of architecture for a castle in the clouds.'

G.K. Chesterton

Planners have a reputation for being unapproachable, but the opposite is true. In fact most will do anything for an easy life – they'd far rather be asked whether something is likely to pass if it means preventing possible court action further down the line. Can you blame them? If your application is refused, and goes to appeal, they risk getting landed with a hefty legal bill.

It isn't necessary to have an application 'in the system' before having discussions with planners; they won't charge for preliminary meetings to discuss what you want to do, so take full advantage. You can also save yourself time and hassle by making a preliminary online enquiry before submitting your full proposal with detailed drawings. This will allow you to gauge a council's reaction to your proposal before you take it any further.

Planning permission rules are open to interpretation. Unlike building regulations, planning regulations differ from one area of the country to the next and the scope for inconsistencies between individual planners – even within one authority – can be huge. The onus is therefore on you and how well you can sell your self-build, renovation or extension project in relation to your particular authority's development plan. A well-crafted design brief doused with 'planning-speak' from your architect is worth its weight in gold and will have considerably more impact than your paint-by-numbers version, particularly if you need to explain away any design deviations. It's also worth getting your neighbours and parish council on side prior to making your application and accommodating any specific concerns they have into your design. It could mean the difference between a quorum approval and a planning committee refusal.

Bottom line: Don't treat your planning officer like a pariah – keep the lines of communication open.

5 Test the mortgage waters with a broker

'The meek may inherit the earth, but the other kind inherits the mortgage.'

Noah Goldstein (academic and scholar)

With more than 5,000 different mortgage products on the UK market, would-be borrowers have their work cut out with lenders to ensure they get the best deal for their circumstances. This scenario is even more acute for those looking to borrow a large percentage of the property's value, which includes cash-strapped first-time buyers.

Contacting high-street lenders direct can get you a more competitive deal, but remember that they'll only be flogging their own limited range of mortgage products, rather than advising on the *best* one for you from across the *whole* market.

Mortgage brokers look in detail at your circumstances and search the market to find a deal that suits you via a 'whole of market' database – software only available to Financial Services Authority (FSA) regulated mortgage advisors. The one caveat, however, is that 'whole of market' excludes direct-to-consumer products, that's to say the handful of major banks like HSBC and its online banking arm First Direct that *only* sell mortgages direct.

All is not lost, however. Just because a broker doesn't earn commission on direct-to-consumer products, doesn't mean they can't give out advice on the different options available. Some will earn their fee by other means, like charging you an amount upfront instead of receiving commission from the lender. That way, you benefit from 'whole of market' advice and the broker can still earn his cut, even if you land up choosing the deal where there's no kickback for them from the lender.

Bottom line: Give yourself a fighting chance and get the full mortgage picture with a broker.

6 Do your due diligence with developers

'The higher the building, the lower the morals.'

Noel Coward

We've all heard horror stories of unscrupulous developers taking deposits for projects that have no planning permission, or even worse, no legal title to the land. So how do you know if you're putting your money in safe hands when you buy off-plan?

Stick to major developers with a proven track record – the best deliver the promised high specification product on time and on budget. Ask about previous developments, visit them and talk to owners.

At the very least, a developer needs sufficient funding in place to cover the costs of buying the land, getting planning permission, designing the project, professional fees and developing the site infrastructure. The best will also have a sizeable chunk put aside to construct and market the properties.

When buying off-plan, a purchase contract can sometimes be passed on or sold to a third party before the unit is completed. In the UK we refer to this as an 'assignable' contract. However, there's a good case to be argued that better developments will not have a high quota of assignable contracts. Banks and developers tend to prefer investors who are there for the long term. A high turnover of assignable contracts during the building stages can severely damage a development's reputation.

What to check

Company registration – the developer should be officially registered at Companies House (*www.companieshouse. gov.uk*) where you can also view their accounts.

Land title confirmation – this ensures that the company is the legal owner of the land and that there are no debts or liens against the land parcel.

Bank guarantee – builders are required to take out a special bank guarantee that will compensate investors should things go wrong. Check this is in place – it will protect your money in the event of a problem.

Planning permission – ask the developer to prove the status of planning permission/building permit.

Build quality guarantee – all good developers offer a guarantee on construction and a detailed quality specification.

Bottom line: Don't sign on the dotted line before your solicitor has carried out full due diligence – it's an extra cost, but worth every penny.

7 Give cowboy builders the heave ho!

'People are always available for work in the past tense.'

Murphy's Law

Cowboy builders can smell easy prey a mile off – so don't put yourself in the firing line by being sloppy with your research. Always check a builder's credentials and never take their word for it; ideally they should be members of the Federation of Master Builders (*www.fmb.co.uk*), the UK's largest building trade organisation.

Be aware of the legal requirements *you* must fulfil when having major improvements done. This is not up to the builder. The work may require Building Regulations approval as well as planning permission – your local council will advise you.

Always put your project out to tender and get a range of quotes. Warning bells should ring for low ones – if you take someone on at an uneconomic price it will be you who loses out if they do a runner halfway through a project. A higher quote doesn't necessarily guarantee the work will be completed within a specified time, but a healthier profit margin means they're more likely to be focusing on your job than a 'rival' project up the road. Always ask to see previous examples of their work and speak to property owners face to face – a phone call isn't enough.

A detailed written contract is an absolute necessity on every job to prevent misunderstandings. The FMB has standard contracts for use by anyone using its recommended builders; this details when payments are due, work schedules, disposal of waste materials and siting of skips.

Dodgy builders trying to get away with sub-standard work rely on property owners being too preoccupied or too green to check work through, so set aside the time to thoroughly understand each job and make frequent on-site visits to monitor progress. If building work isn't your forte, then employ a chartered surveyor to oversee the project for you. They are governed by a code of professional conduct and have compulsory indemnity cover should anything go wrong.

Check that your builder has appropriate insurance, including public liability, to safeguard against any damage done during the building work. It's also a good idea to take out additional insurance to protect your investment. The Master Bond warranty from the FMB provides cover against faulty workmanship and materials as well as structural defects for a fixed number of years.

Bottom line: Hassle-free results don't happen by accident; so agree as much as possible upfront before building starts.

8 Pay for possibilities with an architect

'A building is a string of events belonging together.'

Chris Fawcett (architect)

Most of us wouldn't think twice about shelling out hundreds of pounds on a new carpet, but we'd run a mile at the prospect of paying an architect for his 'advice', writing it off as pure extravagance. With increasing numbers of homeowners opting to improve instead of move, employing an architect could end up being the best money you ever spend. Even if it's a simple extension you're going for, skimping on creative input and going straight to construction means you miss out on a crucial stage in the home-making process – namely, good design. Your builder may well deliver his side of the bargain with a quality construction, but only an architect can fully interpret your ideas. So what precisely are you paying for? In a nutshell, the 'big picture' – the ability to consider many different aspects of a project, from assessing your lifestyle needs and selecting materials to getting round spatial constraints, all set within a workable, budget-conscious timetable.

Bottom line: Set the stage with an architect before jumping into bed with the builder.

4

On the Couch

1 Pitch the price right

'Something you don't want is dear at any price.'

Proverb

The asking price of a property isn't just about comparable values – emotional intelligence has its part to play too. A savvy buyer, for example, will not only look to pin-point a fair market value for a place but also to suss out how much room for manoeuvre there is with the seller. By the same token, 'switched on' vendors, even when they've reached an agreement with their agent on their home's value, are still likely to drop the asking price a little, and not just to entice buyers with a bargain. By adopting this approach, they're tapping into significant 'thresholds', which occur every £10,000 or so. These are price brackets that would-be investors are most likely to put down as their pre-viewing ceiling price. Once they see the property they make an emotional connection to it however, chances are they'll adjust their initial figure upwards – a £5,000 increase can, for example, be qualified as a 'doable' addition in the mortgage.

So, if your property is genuinely worth £360,000, price it at £350,000 – that way you won't scare off buyers who've set £350,000 as their cut-off point; once you've reeled them in, they can potentially be cajoled into spending a little more. An alternative strategy is to put your home on at £359,000. A negligible difference, you might think, but the psychological effect of rounding down the whole number (the 99p effect) can be profound, encouraging potential buyers to still see your house as 'within their means'.

Reversing this scenario and pricing your property one tier higher doesn't reap the same rewards. Put it on at £370,000 and to buyers qualified to purchase at this price point your home won't seem like a bargain; it will merely seem overpriced. As for those qualified to pay £360,000 – what it's actually worth – they'll dismiss it as 'out of their league'.

Bottom line: When selling, fix a price tag that's slightly below a threshold, but close to a property's market value, because everybody likes room to negotiate.

2 Just be yourself

'Never keep up with the Joneses. Always drag them down to your level.'

Quentin Crisp

Society has us wired to be status seekers, to crave things that will make us look good in the eyes of others. To a point, there's nothing wrong with this 'keep up with the Joneses' mindset, especially if it helps our own psychological comfort levels. But once we start looking at potential homes from this prescriptive standpoint, our perspective shifts and we can quickly lose sight of our true needs and wants. Preoccupation with prestige and social standing can ultimately rob us of living the life we really want. So ditch the 'more, better, best' mantra when you're house hunting. It's a brave step to jettison conformist ideas about where we live being a measure of our success, but it's worth doing. Just remember – it's not your image of yourself that has to live in your home, it's *you*.

Bottom line: We all want to fit in, but when it comes to your home, *your* needs come first.

3 Keep your emotions in check

'Comfort in expressing your emotions will allow you to share the best of yourself with others, but not being able to control your emotions will reveal your worst.'

Bryant H. McGill (US poet/author)

'Property lust at first sight' – PLAFS – is a dangerous thing. Why? Because in the first few minutes of viewing a potential new home, your sensory organs go into overdrive – they tell you how you feel and what you want in that moment. Unfortunately, they don't alert you to the potential consequences of satisfying those desires.

It's only after you've moved in that the negatives you chose to ignore begin to surface. You realise that buying that 'bigger' house in a location that adds an hour to your daily commute leaves you too exhausted to enjoy all that 'extra garden'. Buyers who get caught up in the moment quickly discover another downside of PLAFS. The passion is short lived. Once these emotional receptors do their job, they push us to seek a new high somewhere else. So is there any way to escape this dopamine trap?

Our 'gut reaction', which insists on immediate gratification, will always be with us. But you can turn it to your advantage if you can detach yourself long enough to determine the nature of an overwhelming attraction – is it lust or love? If you've fallen for a particular property, ask yourself whether you love the kitchen because of the latest designer appliances and slinky granite or because the layout of the room makes casual dining easier. The house that will make you happiest isn't necessarily the biggest, the most amenity-laden or the one with the party-on patio. It's more likely the place where you can build memories: celebrate life's events – anniversaries, Sunday lunch with the family and barbecues under the brolly.

Bottom line: Emotions run rampant when purchasing property. Keep them in check or you'll be paying the price for years to come.

4 Choose your home – choose your mood

'I keep my personality in a cupboard under the stairs at home, so no one else can see it or nick it.'

Dawn French

Most of us feel some kind of geographical propriety – where you are is a huge part of who you are. Likewise where we come from (or where we've recovered coming from) helps shape our personalities and our value systems. Home is the nerve centre of that feeling; it's our bedrock for sanctuary and security – or at least the desire for it.

Look at Jane Austen's *Pride and Prejudice*. Elizabeth is smitten by Pemberley long before she falls for the smouldering charms of Mr Darcy. And Darcy is ill at ease at Netherfield – it's only when he gets home that he can truly let his guard down. When you start your house-hunting quest picture yourself and your family within those walls and in that neighbourhood. Your surroundings are an extension of yourself, so if they're a fit, you fit. If they're out of kilter, you're going to feel the same.

Wherever you go, you also have to figure out ways to make that place yours. It could mean something as simple as hanging a montage of family photos on your bedroom wall so the first thing you see in the morning are your loved ones, or having a quiet corner where you can wile away an hour kipping on your favourite chair. Maybe it's purging the clutter. Most of us can't have the perfect home, but it's hugely important to make what we have feel comfortable and inviting. You don't need the show-home look, just those things that keep you centred and give you peace of mind.

Bottom line: We're all creatures of our environment – if it feels right, it probably is.

5 Spot the buyer types

'You can tell a lot about a person's character by his way of eating jellybeans.'

Ronald Reagan

Buyers come in all shapes and sizes, but that shouldn't stop you from applying a little kitchen table psychology to ease the negotiation process. Pinpointing individual 'types' can not only boost likely interest levels in your cherished home, it can improve your chances of converting lukewarm browsers into ready-and-willing buyers.

Go-getters – ambitious, family-orientated high-flyers. They want a house that reflects their status – state-of-the-art kitchens, sumptuous bathrooms and outdoor play areas for the kids. They'll appreciate a facts-at-your-fingertips approach – point out key assets, then let your house do the talking.

Real dealers – self-made entrepreneurs and 'creative' business types. They're public spirited and sociable and make great neighbours. They want a place to unwind, a characterful home they can feel a connection to. They enjoy human interaction and will respond well to a personal approach – a welcome handshake, a freshly-brewed cup of coffee. Drop in a few historical snippets about the house and draw their attention to any unusual design features.

Stalwarts – champions of old-school values: heavily into family, and community. They work in banking, law and the public sector, and like a conventional way of life. Traditional, characterful properties fit the bill. Less daring in their personality type, they respond well to supportive chat and reassurance – highlight the security of the neighbourhood, the friendly neighbours and the low-maintenance garden.

Trendies – young and upwardly mobile on the lower rungs of the property ladder, they know what they want and have a game plan to get there. Their ideal home? A new-build townhouse or apartment in a convenient urban location. Sell them the lifestyle. Point out 'status features' such as wireless Internet, roof-top garden, mood lighting – if it's an inexpensive home in a desirable neighbourhood you're selling then you're on to a winner.

Keep-it-uppers – school leavers who have gone straight into the world of work. Their ideal property is a below-market-value 'fixer-upper' with garden, close to a town or city centre. Highlight the property's financial potential and inexpensive ways they can add value.

Bottom line: Understanding your buyer can mean the difference between a 'thanks, but no thanks' and 'we'll take it' – so get the low-down before the viewing merry-go-round begins.

6 Keep your sanity and get a man cave

'All marriages are happy. It's the living together after-wards that causes all the trouble.'

Raymond Hull *(Canadian writer)*

Every man needs a nag-free zone, a place to scratch, to day-dream, and escape the fragrant onslaught of femininity. A recent survey revealed that over 50 per cent of men find it 'enriching' to have a quiet place to escape to in the house – personal space where they can revel in Neanderthal manliness. And that's no bad thing. The old saying 'familiarity breeds contempt' is as relevant today as it's ever been. Based on the premise that in many homes the woman takes charge of running the entire house just the way she likes, finding your partner a sliver of space to call his own can make the difference between his and hers strife and harmonious living. Acknowledging that you value time apart isn't a black mark against your relationship; it's a common sense step towards a happy ever after.

Bottom line: Women have their baths; men have their man caves – so keep the beer and bubbles flowing.

7 Make your house a home

'Home is a place you grow up wanting to leave and grow old wanting to get back to.'

John Ed Pearce (Pulitzer Prize-winning journalist)

Home means different things to different people. It can be a haven, a roof over our heads or, to quote Bob Dylan, a 'shelter from the storm'. Over the last few decades we've promoted property to the status of a glorified piggy bank – a national hubris that has led us to treat our homes like substitute credit cards, equity cakes sliced to finance our every need from exotic holidays and new cars to cushy retirement plans. And herein lies the danger. Property certainly brings financial kudos – there aren't, after all, many things that can put a six-figure cheque in your pocket when you sell them. But by viewing your pad as *just* an investment vehicle, you're losing sight of its primary role as a cherished home. When you think about it, by the time you've shelled out on repairs, and renovations, and paid your taxes and insurance, your property has probably sapped much of what you'd make in pure profit anyway. So try adjusting your mindset. Reappraise where you live for its intangible rather than financial returns: a space that contributes to your well-being; a place of inspiration and affirmation – that's where the *real* gains are to be made.

Bottom line: Your home is a nest, not a nest egg – so put your feet up and enjoy!

8 Opt for a win-win outcome

'One should always play fair when one has the winning cards.'

Oscar Wilde

Real estate negotiations don't have to be a close combat affair if you abide by the golden rule of give and take. The ultimate goal is ensuring that both sides have a good feeling about the deal on the table. The crucial point, however, is its perceived deal – it doesn't have to mirror reality. As long as the buyer and seller *feel* the final offer is fair, they're happy. It's human nature after all – whenever we make a major purchase we like to be seen to have behaved wisely and done the best we could.

So don't back your buyer or vendor into a corner – stay flexible. Find out what makes them tick. Sometimes it's not all about money. Very often it's the small concessions that carry sway: the seller might want to move swiftly or the buyer might need extra time to make relocation arrangements. If you've gotten most of what you want and the other party is trying to wangle a few extras, then go with it, so they too can sense some 'victory' in the bargaining process. If they perceive to be getting what they want, the deal will be less likely to fall through at the last minute. Pride can be a deal breaker, so take time to study the bigger picture. Do you have a good feeling about the offer? If yes, then go for it.

Bottom line: Property negotiations require give and take

– keep a few 'concession tricks' up your sleeve and you're more likely to get what you want.

5

Money Matters

Mortgage: a house with a guilty conscience.

Anon

1 Navigate the mortgage minefield

To fix or not to fix is the perennial quandary facing today's mortgage shoppers as no one, not even the most gifted of crystal ball gazers, can predict the path of interest rates. In an ideal world, we'd all be sitting pretty on cushy short-term mortgage deals. There's a certain freedom that comes from not being locked into a longer-term fixed rate and knowing that, should interest rates fall, we can quickly switch products to suit. Ultimately, however, the smart choice is the one that best meets our financial needs, and, as we all know, rates can go up as well as down.

The 'steady Eddies' of the mortgage world, **fixed-rate mortgages**, are the product of choice of risk-averse buyers including first-timers, as well as those looking to secure a high loan-to-value deal. Homeowners know what's expected of them for the term of the arrangement, including how much they need to shell out in monthly repayments. Rates are fixed for an agreed period, usually between two to five years, but can potentially run for the entire duration of the mortgage, allowing you to plan for the future with confidence. Fixed-raters don't get off scot-free, however. Certainty comes at a price, in the form of upfront fees and early redemption charges. Moreover, once the fixed period has finished, borrowers often end up on the lender's more expensive standard variable rate (SVR), and may be locked into it, which is a future cost to be factored in at the time of the deal. If interest rates do fall, you'll also miss out on any reduction in your repayments.

For those with the financial headroom to manage potential repayment rises, a **variable-rate mortgage** (VRM) could work out the better option. The absence of mortgage arrangement fees means VRMs usually start off cheaper to begin with, ideal if low payments in the near term are your primary requirement or if you don't plan to live in the property long enough for interest rates to rise. On the downside, your monthly repayments are likely to fluctuate over the life of the loan, so unless you have a comfy financial buffer, you run the risk of losing what you gained from that tempting introductory rate.

Whichever product you choose, the key figure to keep your eye on is the standard variable rate (SVR) – the rate that lenders base their products on and the one that you will be charged once any 'introductory discount rate' has expired. These days, borrowers are spending much longer periods paying their lender's more expensive SVR because of the shortage of alternative products on the market, an inevitable side effect of the crash. That said, if you're coming to the end of a fixed rate mortgage or another tied-in period, and have a decent deposit or equity in your home (around 25 per cent) and a fault-free credit rating, you should still be able to secure a better deal by shopping around. Always ask for two mortgage illustrations, one with, and one without arrangement fees. This will allow you to fully assess the total cost of your mortgage before making a switch.

Bottom line: Choosing the right mortgage boils down to one simple question: will you be able to cope with higher payments if interest rates rise? Switching to a pricier fixed rate may go against your instincts, but you're making sure you know what's in store.

2 Check the small print

'The big print giveth and the small print taketh away.'

Tom Waits

Mortgage lenders are adept at sneaking in 'little extras', a sleight of hand that continues to catch buyers unawares; so if you've whittled down your choice of mortgage options to two or three possibles, go back and check for the following small print stings:

Early repayment charges – most mortgage companies levy some kind of fixed penalty if you decide to switch to a different provider before the end of your existing deal period. More often than not, this will mean shelling out several months' worth of interest to your lender. If you received cash back when you took out your mortgage, a significant percentage, if not all, of this amount will also have to be paid back. This means that the combined fees charged by both your existing and new lender could cancel out any savings you actually make on the new rate. So how do you know whether to switch or stick? First, do your sums and work out how much you would save in monthly repayments over the term of the new deal. Subtract the early repayment charge (ERC) and any additional fees from this figure. The number you're left with will either be a saving or a loss.

Extended redemption penalties – some mortgage providers try to wangle a little extra income by throwing in an extended redemption tie-in, which requires you to stay with that lender for a fixed period – usually several years – *after* a fixed or capped rate period has expired. This means that any savings made by you during this fixed-rate period could subsequently be wiped out by the rate payable for the remaining years of the deal. Always check 'lock-in' fees with a lender before signing anything.

Exit fee – don't make the fatal error of assuming that this charge is the same as an early repayment charge. It's not. Some lenders automatically charge an additional fee for parting company with them, which they explain away as essential 'administration costs' involved with closing down the mortgage account. If your mortgage provider is unwilling to negotiate on this payment, take it up with the Financial Services Authority (FSA) *www.fsa.gov.uk* – you've nothing to lose.

Higher lending charges – as frustrating as it may be – putting down anything less than a ten per cent deposit on a property these days will result in a higher lending charge or, a mortgage indemnity guarantee (MIG). In a nutshell, this single-premium insurance policy is designed to protect the lender – *not you* – in the event of your property being repossessed and sold for less than the outstanding mortgage. Even more galling – it costs a packet. So if you expect to be slapped with a MIG by your lender, go back and redo your sums; check and see if there's any way of borrowing a larger amount towards your deposit rather than incur the cost of a MIG.

Mortgage payment protection insurance – not without its merits, MPPI still remains a tricky area. If you fall behind on your mortgage repayments and are unable to make good the shortfall, MPPI will cover you for accident, sickness and unemployment but only for a specific period (usually 12 months) and usually with a number of pre-existing medical exclusions such as stress or back problems. Most companies won't allow you to make a claim until 30 to 60 days after the policy was taken out and payments are only covered for a fixed amount per month – around £1,500 to £2,000, which is of little comfort to those with hefty mortgages. To secure the best policy for you, seek advice from an independent financial advisor rather than your mortgage lender or the high street banks. It will mean paying a fee for their services, but it's still likely to work out cheaper than your lender's policy.

Bottom line: Small print can cost you dear – so get your mortgage magnifying glass out.

3 Don't rule out rentals

'When I was kidnapped, my parents snapped into action. They rented out my room.'

Woody Allen

Good times or bad, the desire for home ownership remains deeply ingrained in the British psyche: a rite of passage that nearly 70 per cent of us now enjoy. The emotional nesting pull is irrefutable. It's hard to beat that sense of belonging, however illusory, that comes with calling a place your own.

The minority alternative is renting, which despite the well-versed argument that it's dead money can at times pay dividends. True, as a mere tenant you'll never experience the profit 'highs' that buying and selling can deliver, but you also won't end up knee deep in negative equity, trapped by a loan that's bigger than your house value.

In tough economic times, when rental yields fall, eager landlords will happily sign up to deals that run for several years, a window of opportunity that allows you as a tenant to save up for a deposit on a home of your own. If you're a first-time buyer, it's the perfect scenario – you can work towards that purchase without stepping out of your financial comfort zone. What you lose in permanence over the short-term, you gain in future flexibility.

For others, renting is a calculated move, a breathing space between selling and buying the next house. In a wavering market where prices are falling it can buy you time till they bottom out. Lets between one and six months may cost considerably more than a standard long-term rent, but they often come with all-inclusive perks like prepaid utility bills and private parking. Best of all, they allow you to strike when the time to buy is right.

Bottom line: Renting isn't always money down the drain – it can free up your finances to invest somewhere better when the time is right.

4 Review your house insurance

'Insurance is like marriage. You pay, you pay, you pay and you never get anything back.'

Al Bundy (Married ... with Children)

Mortgage lenders have a reputation for charging hefty commissions on home insurance policies, though adverse press coverage in recent years has stamped out the worst excesses of this practice. Don't be surprised if your lender tries to coerce you into taking out *their* insurance as part of the mortgage deal; some will even add to this pressure by levying a 'get-out' fee for using an alternative provider (which they're legally entitled to do). Nine times out of ten, however, you'll still be better off going elsewhere. Many rival firms will even pay the exit fee on your behalf to secure your business.

Compare what insurance policies are on the market on sites like *www.moneysupermarket.com* and *www. gocompare.com*. Firms apply different underwriting criteria when assessing home cover quotes, so make sure you're comparing like for like on both building and contents insurance.

Building insurance – don't make the mistake of supplying the market value of your home to the insurer, rather than the amount it would cost to rebuild your home from scratch (the market value is much higher). To find your rebuild costs, simply refer back to your original mortgage documents or to one of the many property comparison websites that offer a special conversion table produced by BCIS (the Building Cost Information Service), or you can register direct with *www.bcis.co.uk* to access their quick-check online service.

Contents insurance – fit a burglar alarm, approved window locks and smoke detectors and you could shave as much as five per cent off your premium. The same applies to time-switch lights and outdoor security lighting.

Covering your possessions for accidental damage – known as 'all risks extension' – will add a sizeable chunk to your premium. So, if you're unlikely to go through the rigmarole of claiming for wine stains on your beloved shag pile or casserole burns on the kitchen work surface, then leave this off.

Many companies now offer a no-claims discount for 'careful' policy holders – the fewer the claims, the lower your premium. If it's a small claim, it's often better to settle this yourself than claim on your insurance, as it will up your premium for the ensuing year.

Bottom line: Home insurance is a highly competitive market and companies will work hard to win your custom – make the most of it.

5 Mine the cash in your home

'Don't stay in bed, unless you can make money in bed.'

George Burns

Need extra cash to help pay the bills? Then give the following moneymaking schemes a whirl:

Get a lodger – the 'Rent a Room' scheme set up by the Government allows you to make £4,250 a year tax-free by renting furnished accommodation in your main home, though you won't be able to claim expenses like heating and lighting. Try flat share websites such as *www.spareroom.co.uk* and *www.gumtree.com.* If you live in a university town, register your details with the college's accommodation officer. Always get references and have a written tenant agreement about extra bills, off-limit areas and house rules.

Be a Monday–Friday landlord – growing in popularity in commuter belt areas, weekday-only lodgers allow you to have the best of both worlds: earn an income *and* get your spare room back at the weekends. Try *www.mondayto friday.com* and *www.yours2share.com.*

Host a foreign student – overseas students, keen to brush up on their English, often prefer the home comforts of a 'host' family to going it alone in a bed-sit. Some only stay a couple of weeks, others a year or more, but it can earn you between £100 and £350 per week depending on the location and size of your property. One of the benefits of hosting is the flexibility it provides – you can do as little or as much as you want during the calendar year. Contact your local education authority or the International Association of Language Centres *www.ialc.org.*

Bring a little Hollywood into your home – allowing a film crew into your home for a few days can be a lucrative way to make some extra cash, with daily rates in the region of £300 to upwards of £1,000 if you have a home with particularly distinctive features. Contact the BBC locations department, your local film commission or one of the national location libraries in London. You can also register your home on *www.amazingspace.co.uk,* which hosts an online library of properties. Other sites accessed by directors and location managers include *www.locationpartnership.com* and *www.locations-uk.com.*

Park your assets – if you live in a city and don't mind someone parking their wheels on your driveway every morning, then why not rent it out? Rental periods can be just a few hours, or daily, so you can soon rack up a regular income stream. Always draw up a contract, tell your insurance company and check that the driver has insurance to cover you for accidental damage. Visit *www.parkatmyhouse.com, www.letalife.com* and *www.parklet.co.uk.*

Cultivate your garden – if you have a plot of land going spare or a sliver of garden you're happy to part with, then you could consider selling it off to a developer, or, if time and cash flow permit, applying for planning permission and building on it yourself. Advertise your plot on *www.uklanddirectory.org.uk*

Make some space – self-storage is big business these days, so if you've got an empty garage, garden shed or lock-up that's crying out to be filled, place an ad in your local rag and pass the word round that you've space to spare. Always draw up a garage rental agreement. A template can be found on the Landlord Protection Agency website *www.thelpa.com.*

Bottom line: Get your home earning its keep and get creative with your ideas.

6 Avoid negative equity

'Never run into debt. Not if you can find anything else to run into.'

Josh Billings (19th-century humourist)

A harsh reminder of the reckless noughties, negative equity, continues to blight the lives of thousands of homeowners in the UK, particularly those who banked on house price growth to help them pay off their mortgage. So what practical steps can you take to minimise your exposure?

Reduce your debt – most mortgages will allow you to repay up to ten per cent without incurring penalty charges, but even smaller reductions can help build up the amount of equity you have in your home.

Switch to a repayment mortgage – those who've signed up to an interest-only mortgage are more likely to feel the effects of house prices falls because lenders will expect the full mortgage amount back when you sell your house. Any fall in value therefore needs to be covered by you, potentially landing you in debt. If you can, consider switching to a repayment mortgage. Your outgoings will be bigger in the short term, but long term, you're likely to make that back and more besides.

Start saving – prepare yourself for higher monthly repayments by building up a lump sum in a savings account to make up the shortfall when you sell or remortgage. Find out how much extra you're likely to have to pay and put that difference aside in a tax-free cash Individual Savings Account (ISA). Starting to save before the payment shock hits will enable you to budget in advance.

Be upfront with your lender – repossession in lenders' eyes is very much a last resort. It's a costly procedure: they have to sell the property and realise their loss as well as yours. So if you sense trouble ahead, get in early with some practical suggestions – guidelines from the Financial Services Authority (*www.fsa.gov.uk*) will help you present workable alternatives, such as lower monthly repayments now with the balance being added to the loan.

Bottom line: when the going gets tough don't bury your head in the financial sandpit – take action.

7 Get energy efficient

'The time to save is now. When a dog gets a bone, he doesn't go out and make a down-payment on a bigger bone, he buries the one he's got.'

Will Rogers (comedian)

If the only time you get an inkling of how much energy you're burning up around the home is by the scorch marks on the carpet when your monthly bills come through the letter-box, then it might be time to rethink your approach.

Do an audit – the Energy Saving Trust offers a free online energy check – it takes minutes to do and you could shave as much as £250 per annum off your household bills. Go to *www.energysavingtrust.org.uk*.

Read your meter – avoid having an 'E' for estimate next to your gas or electricity meter reading. Why risk an overestimate and have your money sitting in your supplier's bank instead of earning interest in yours? Always take your meter reading every time you get a bill and advise your company straightaway if there's a discrepancy.

Switch supplier – call your supplier and ask for your annual energy consumption in kilowatt-hours. You can then compare what you're paying against rival companies on comparison websites such as *www.uswitch.com*, *www.moneysupermarket.com* and *www.theenergyshop.com*. Remember that buying your gas and electricity from the same supplier and taking advantage of a 'dual fuel' agreement can usually secure you a good discount. Likewise, paying by direct debit can save you as much as ten per cent.

Water – no one likes to pour money down the drain, but before you consider installing a water meter, log onto the Consumer Council for Water's website (*www.water.org.uk*) or the water regulator Ofwat (*www.ofwat.gov.uk*) and complete their online test to find out if it's worth your while switching. The rule of thumb is that if there are more bedrooms than people in your home, then a meter will save you money – as much as £200 off your annual bill. All's not lost, however, if you switch to a meter and find that you're not happy with the change. You can always revert back to unmeasured charging within 12 months.

If you don't have a water meter installed, reducing hot water use is one of the key ways to cut gas and electricity bills. It's generally cheaper to heat water only when you require it. If a cylinder is properly lagged, hot water will stay hot for a good ten to twelve hours, so set your boiler for times when you need to draw off large amounts of hot water. If you haven't got a cylinder thermostat then ask your plumber to fit one; you'll recoup the costs in a relatively short space of time.

Heating – setting your thermostat just one degree down can save you up to ten per cent on your fuel bill.

Make sure you have control over the time your central heating goes on and off – try setting your system to come on about 45 minutes before you get up and go off half an hour after bedtime.

Insulating your loft is one of the most worthwhile ways of preventing heat from escaping. Twenty-five per cent of heat loss is through the roof. Up to 35 per cent of heat in a home is lost through the walls, so filling cavity walls is another excellent preventive measure.

Lighting – the cost of lighting an average home has risen by a massive 15 per cent over the past two years, according to a recent government survey. Switching to energy-efficient light bulbs can cut wastage by over three-quarters, while switching off appliances like TVs and PCs at the mains instead of leaving them on standby can shave a further hundred pounds or so off your annual bill.

Bottom line: Get energy efficient – it means extra money in the bank and a greener living environment.

8 Check your council tax

'Taxes grow without rain.'

Jewish proverb

When the council tax system was established in 1993, properties were placed in bands from A to H based on assessments made in 1991. Amazingly, most properties haven't been reassessed since, though official records indicate that one in twenty homes have subsequently been found to be in too high a council tax band.

If you think you may be paying too much or have recently moved into a new home and want to double-check your banding, ask your neighbours who have similar properties and see what they're paying. You can also verify the banding of any property by logging onto the Valuation Office Agency web site (*www.voa.gov.uk*), or *www.saa.gov.uk* in Scotland. If you discover neighbours with a similar property in a lower band, then you may have a claim.

Certain council taxpayers are also eligible for special discounts or exemptions:

- If you're a single occupant or share your home with someone who is aged 18 or over (excluding your partner) you could save up to 25 per cent per annum off your bill. This also applies to full-time students and those on a low income.

- For unoccupied and unfurnished properties, which need renovation to make them habitable, you can claim Council Tax exemption for the first 12 months, and for any length of time after that you may claim up to 50 per cent off the normal rate (although this does depend on which council you're in), based on their 'long-term empty' policy.

- If you have a second home, you can also claim a discount of between ten and fifty per cent at the discretion of the appropriate council. Banding appeals can be made online at the Valuation Office Agency, or alternatively homeowners can write to their local authority's listing assessor.

Bottom line: Check your council banding – one phone call could drop you a band and get you a backdated settlement.

6

Different Strokes

'When you're a successful bidder it means you're prepared to spend more money than anyone else. I'm not sure if that's congratulations or condolences.'

Eli Broad (US philanthropist)

1 Get in on the auction

With over 30,000 properties sold under the hammer at discounts of up to 40 per cent, it's no wonder increasing numbers of house hunters are scouting the auction rooms for property bargains. One of the key attractions is that it's a 'fair play' process – you can see when the bids go in and, as such, it's an open competition. Property lots range from family 'fixer-uppers' to period properties and smallholdings. The majority are on the market due to bankruptcy, repossession or to clear debts. Guide prices can, however, fall shy of the final sales price, depending on the interest displayed on the day and any offers received in the run-up to the sale, so keeping your budget in mind when the bidding one-upmanship gathers pace in the auction room is vital.

Most auction houses hold sales throughout the year and will post dates in the local paper, but you can also get advance notice of UK-wide sales by registering with the property auction information service website run by the Essential Information Group (*www.eigroup.co.uk*).

If a particular property catches your eye, the next step is to appoint a solicitor to check the document pack relating to your lot. This includes the key searches but no in-depth survey or valuation. View the property several times prior to auction and have a structural survey undertaken, particularly if it's an older home. Sound out local agents and see what similar properties are going for and then talk to your bank. Your lender must also be aware of and able to meet the strict auction deadlines by giving you an offer of a mortgage before the sale. If you can't secure this in time, don't bid.

On auction day, try and resist the temptation to open the bidding on your lot, as this can push up the price – wait for someone else to start the ball rolling. If you're the last and highest bidder when the auctioneer's hammer falls, then the property's yours. At this point you're legally committed to completing the sale, with the same legal implications as a signed contract. You can expect to pay ten per cent of the cost of the property before you leave the auction and settle the balance within 28 days. As speedy a process as it is, buying at auction doesn't exempt you from any of the normal purchase fees, including stamp duty. The auctioneer will also require a buyer's premium equivalent to 1.5 per cent of the sale price, with an administration fee, typically in the region of £200.

Top Tips

- Get a feel for the auction process by sitting in on a few.

- Getting cold feet after a bid has been accepted can cost you dearly – you not only stand to lose your deposit, you also risk being taken to court by the vendor and forced to pay their expenses and the difference in the price if they eventually end up selling their place for less.

- Don't give up hope if the property you're after fails to reach its reserve price and goes unsold. If your bid is close enough, the vendor may decide to accept your offer post-auction.

Bottom line: Auctions are a great place to pick up a bargain – always stick to your budget and understand the market you're buying in.

2 Don't rule out repossessions

'Opportunity often comes disguised in the form of misfortune.'

Napoleon Hill (US author)

Buying a repossessed property has unpleasant connotations for some, yet it can help put a debt-ridden vendor back on the road to recovery, as well as proving a savvy purchase, with some homes selling for up to 40 per cent off their market value. So how do you go about tracking one down?

Estate agents often get first crack at marketing repossessions but don't openly advertise their 'status', so you'll need to make a direct approach and see what they have listed as 'vacant property', 'no chain' or 'sealed bids'. Even more than a 'normal' sale, the property needs to prove itself to you. If the vendor has been trying to sell the place for some time, there's a good chance you'll uncover defects, so bring along someone you trust to give the house the once over and get a survey done on older properties.

If you put in an offer on a place and it's accepted, don't take it personally if it remains on the market. A bank or building society has a legal obligation to secure as much as possible for the property to recoup losses and they may even advertise the house in the local newspapers as a 'notice of offer' in the hope of getting a better price, which they're legally within their rights to do. If you're not prepared to run the risk of being gazumped, then buying a repo is probably not for you.

Top Tips

- Contact local agents and auction houses and ask to be put on their mailing lists for 'distress sales'.

- Keep an eye out in your local paper for 'notice of offer' adverts – if it states 'by order of the mortgagees in possession', you know it's a repossession.

- Always have 'subject to contract and without prejudice' written into any bid you make – this will protect you against any hitches that might arise before exchange of contracts.

Bottom line: If you can act quickly and are a dab hand at doing your due diligence, repossessions are worth pursuing.

3 Surf the Internet swap-shop

'True love is like a pair of socks. You've gotta have two and they've gotta match.'

Anon

Billed as the 'matchmaking' service for bricks and mortar, home exchange websites offer an online meeting point for homeowners looking to advertise their property, find a suitable match and do a swap. The benefits are clear – you not only cut out the middleman, but you also avoid hefty agency fees. Successful swapping does, however, require an open-minded approach and a degree of compromise on the house spec and location.

To maximise your chances of finding a match, spread your net as wide as you can by registering with several of the main sites including *www.easyhouseexchange.com* and *www.thepropertyswap.com*. Most offer a fixed fee (in the region of £20-£40) for a three-month subscription. Full details of your property are required together with a description of the type of home you're looking for, price range and preferred locations. The database will then automatically search for suitable matches. If a suitable swap comes up, vendor and buyer can contact one another via the site and arrange viewings. If both parties are happy with what they see, you'll be left to continue the process independently with the swap unfolding like a standard real estate transaction.

While home exchange certainly cuts down on the expense of using intermediaries, it doesn't exempt you from any of the usual fees or taxes including conveyancing and stamp duty. Before you make an offer, speak to local agents and confirm market values of similar properties in the area. Have a survey done and visit the property at least twice. In a case where there's a price differential between the two homes, this can usually be met with either a cash payment, or by new finance from a mortgage lender. Many lenders will also allow a transfer of your mortgage from your old property to your new one, subject to a satisfactory valuation.

Bottom line: Home exchange is unlikely to find you the *perfect* house match, but for buyers willing to take a gamble, you just might uncover a gem.

4 Nimble up with new-build

'It's only the modern that ever becomes old-fashioned.'

Oscar Wilde

Go back a decade or so and buyer types were easy to peg. Die-hard traditionalists had a penchant for inglenook fireplaces and chunky beams; while move-with-the-times modernists championed the easy-care attributes of new-build. For contemporary fans, character properties equated to a lifetime of big bills and drafty rooms, while new-builds were typecast as faceless and bland by the old school. Thankfully times have moved on, with a softening of attitudes fashioned by a new generation of property styles and designs. Now, with the government committed to easing the UK's housing shortage by 2016, the number of new-build properties is set to far outrank the number of traditional homes on the open market.

So what are the upsides of buying new?

- You can kiss goodbye to chains, blind bidding and gazumping.

- Property styles cover the whole spectrum from cosy flats, spacious penthouses and loft conversions to mock period mansions and eco-friendly homes. Design layouts also have specific buyers in mind – singles, families or couples, with square footage flexibility you'd struggle to find in an older home.

- New-build homes are on average four times more energy efficient than older homes. Most come with insulation and double glazing as standard. Some even offer a 'green' choice with solar-powered heating and built-in water saving features, saving you hundreds of pounds on your household bills. Repairs and maintenance costs will also be kept to a minimum with no faulty electrics, leaky roofs or rotting windows to attend to.

- Buy a new-build and you get a ten-year build warranty from the NHBC (National House Building Council), or other insurer, one that's likely to include smoke alarms, high performance locks, burglar alarms and security lighting. Standard developer extras also include fixtures and fittings, carpets and white goods.

What to check

- New-builds market at a significant premium – so always compare existing property prices in your chosen area, and shop around with other developers/builders.

- Beware of 'cash incentives' such as deposit and stamp duty paid, or cash towards your mortgage payment; you'll still have to shell out this money first, as it's only redeemable upon completion of the sale.

- Don't fall head over heels for the show home – the look-don't-touch kitchens and high-spec bathrooms are likely to be upgraded versions of the standard offering. Different house builders offer different extras so find out *exactly* what's thrown in as part of the deal. Add-on costs such as carpets, curtains and flooring can quickly mount up.

- Buying new means a chain-free purchase, but you'll still have your builder's schedule to comply with. You'll be expected to put down a reservation deposit, sort out your mortgage and exchange contracts within a month. If you're buying off-plan (before building work is complete), delays are not uncommon. Contracts normally specify that completion is 'on notice' – sometimes several weeks after building work is completed.

- Recently completed homes can have 'snags', minor defects such as leaky taps and ill-fitting doors that remain after the building has been signed off. The NHBC ten-year warranty only covers major structural issues, so where possible get a deadline for remedying snags written into the contract.

Bottom line: Period properties might be our architectural heritage, but new-build is the future – embrace it for gain.

5 Get more for less with fractionals

'My idea of heaven is a great big baked potato and someone to share it with.'

Oprah Winfrey

If you've toyed with the idea of purchasing a second home, but ruled it out in the likelihood of limited use and high overheads, then fractional ownership might be just what you're looking for. Unlike timeshare, which offers 'vacation time only', fractional ownership confers a deeded interest and equity share in a managed property; in short, all the benefits of a holiday home for several weeks a year, but bought in partnership with others who bear the costs with you. Property that would otherwise be sold outright can be purchased in multiples; the number of shares offered principally a function of the amount of prime time that can be guaranteed.

Prices vary based on the size, amenities and location of the individual property and start from as little as £30,000 plus annual fees to upwards of £300,000. Property is usually of a high standard, fully furnished with administration and maintenance provided by a professional management team. Owners, in turn, have full rights of ownership, including selling to others, renting, buying additional fractional shares and/or upgrading to outright ownership, with a fraction becoming part of the owner's portfolio of heritable wealth. For further information go to *www.rocksureproperty.com* and *www.fractionallife.com*.

How can you ensure you 'buy wise' in the fractional property market?

- Research the market – buying a quarter share of a well-located high-end property can often yield better capital appreciation than an outright purchase in a lesser price bracket.

- Ensure that all 'on costs' (property taxes, insurance and maintenance) are budgeted for and written into the deed of co-ownership contract and that a full property management service is included in your purchase.

- Multiple ownership tax issues can be complex so take advice from a specialist lawyer. Buyers should also have contracts checked to ensure clean and legal title, an equitable stake in the property and no restrictions to selling shares on the open market.

- Loans for fractional schemes are scarce – owners usually buy outright, although it's possible to remortgage your main property. Make sure your mortgage debt is below 75 per cent of your home's value.

Bottom line: If part investment, part pleasure is your motivation for owning a second home then fractional ownership may well fit the bill.

6 Part exchange for gain

'He who seeks for gain must be at some expense.'

Plautus (Roman playwright)

Pioneered by Barratt Homes in the 1970s, part exchange is now a common investment tool used to shift new homes in the £200,000 to £400,000 price bracket, yet many people are still unaware of its existence. To be eligible, you have to be an 'upwardly mobile' homeowner; that's to say, looking to move up the housing ladder and specifically to a new-build property. A developer will usually arrange for at least two independent valuations of your existing home before making you an offer based on those estimates. If you accept the offer, subject to satisfactory surveys, the development company then becomes your buyer, freeing you up to put in a confirmed offer on your chosen new-build home. Every developer works slightly differently, but common stipulations include the value of your existing property not exceeding 70 per cent of the value of your new home, and the exclusion of certain home types such as studio flats. Your existing property also needs to be in good nick – anything deemed unsuitable will be brought to your attention in the survey, allowing you to rectify it or you will have to accept a lower offer price from the developer.

On the surface, part exchange clearly has its merits, enabling you to move into a spanking new home in record time without the hassle of a chain or years of DIY to bring the place up to scratch. But the concept isn't entirely catch free. The offer price on your existing property from the developer should be a 'fair valuation' based on several independent quotes and a good developer will be able to give you a reasoned explanation as to how they arrived at their offer price. But even with a decent offer, you can still only expect on average 75 to 85 per cent of your home's market value (90 per cent tops in a strong market).

Tempting introductory offers may also weaken your resolve and get you signing up before you assess the deal in detail. A classic is the 'move in for £100' offer. As great as it may sound, this set-up invariably requires payment upfront of a deposit, plus legal fees and stamp duty. Some purchases also come with the restriction 'on selected plots' and these are likely to be the locations that have been hardest to shift. It's also important to check what stage the development has got to in terms of completion. If it already has resales on offer, ask local agents whether the price they're fetching matches the developer's asking price. You may discover that, even taking into account the discounts on offer, an older home works out better value.

Bottom line: Part exchange can be a great way of trading up if property valuation keeps pace with inflation, but only if you time it right and choose your development wisely.

7 Think out of the house-buying box

'If you're not willing to risk the unusual, you'll have to settle for the ordinary.'

Jim Rohn (US entrepreneur and author)

Most house purchases adhere to 'two-up-two-down' convention. But by widening your buying horizons you could land up with the 'ideal' home that invigorates your mind as well as your finances. True, your average high-street bank is likely to turn you down flat on a loan for a roofless wreck no matter how much 'raw potential' it has, but there are still exceptions to the rule with specialist lenders dealing in marine finance, renovations and self-build projects happy to target the weird and the wonderful.

Houseboats – growing in popularity as trendy, affordable bases, the average floating home will set you back around £60,000 and can be funded by a 'marine mortgage' available from specialist lenders. Purchasers require at least a 20 per cent deposit and loans tend to come with a 15-year maximum term on a repayment basis. Additional costs include maintenance (around £1,000 a year), residential mooring, which will vary according to the river location and council tax (for urban locations), which is payable at the lowest banding (A).

Bespoke conversions – that crumbling chapel or windswept barn might be a luxurious Shangri-La by the time you've worked your DIY magic, but at the moment it's more down-and-out ruin than stately pile. A derelict shell doesn't offer the lender much to go on. A small number of lenders specialise in extreme make-overs including Norwich and Peterborough Building Society, the Ecology Building Society and Buildstore (*www.buildstore.co.uk*). Loans are paid on a staged basis – first the price of the derelict building or a percentage of its value. A valuer will then come and check that it has reached an appropriate level of building standard before the next sum is released and so on. The Society for the Protection of Ancient Buildings (*www.spab.org.uk*) publishes a quarterly magazine listing of old buildings for sale and in need of repair from cottages to castles.

Outbuildings – these days, garages can be converted into domestic dwellings without planning permission, although you should contact your local authority before going ahead as exceptions to the rule still apply. Get your solicitor to check paperwork and inform the Land Registry. In some instances, land on which a garage is built isn't registered. In this instance, your solicitor can carry out a conveyance instead. Don't forget to set aside funds for a refit – how much you spend should be relative to what you expect to get back on future resale.

Self-build – buying a plot of land to self-build is one of the few remaining ways to make a decent profit from property. It may sound daunting, but you don't need to be a DIY guru to embrace the self-build world; good organisational skills and time management are just as, if not more important, not to mention having a little vision. Typical plots sell for anything between £80,000 and £100,000 and many for considerably less. The profit from buying land and building a home yourself is typically 30 per cent, added to which you'll have a property that is exactly to your spec and finish. Remember that project managing a home from scratch will eat up a lot of your time; most, however, find the hard work more than worth the challenge.

Bottom line: Four walls don't make a home – you do.

8 Adopt the less is more approach

'My room is so small, the mice are hunchbacked.'

Henny Youngman (British comedian)

The clarion call to consumers is 'bigger is better', but the housing market has become so unwieldy precisely because of our desire for more legroom – it's a quirk of human nature. Wouldn't it be better instead to question what we *really* get out of all that extra space? And why is it that when we downsize, and learn to live within our diminutive means, it can actually end up being a huge relief?

House purchases are usually sparked by life changes – be it the patter of tiny feet, a promotion or impending retirement. While it's generally accepted that we all want to be climbing the property ladder, there are times when actually stepping back a couple of rungs makes more sense, particularly if it ensures that your home becomes a true reflection of your current and future aspirations. Downsize your square footage and you can upgrade your lifestyle; put aside that extra capital for a rainy day or realise a lifetime ambition. Alternatively, you could purchase a smaller house for the same value as your current property, but upgrade to a more desirable neighbourhood. A smaller home doesn't have to be a compromise. You don't need to skimp on the size of the main rooms – you simply opt for fewer of them. So how can you make downsizing the smart choice for you?

Prioritise function – make a list of the rooms you have

94

and when and how often you use them; you may find you can get away with less space and have a layout that's better suited to your everyday needs, e.g. trading that formal dining-room you use once in a blue moon for a bigger kitchen with heaps of storage space.

Crunch the numbers – work out just how much you'd save by trading down. This includes difference in monthly mortgage repayments, utility bills and taxes.

Evaluate the trade-offs – monetary gain alone can't seal the deal. It's important to consider how downsizing will impact on your life. You may, for example, be working round the clock to support a lifestyle that's not ultimately satisfying – if it is, then it's time to think again.

Take action – draw up a wish list of 'no-goes' in a smaller home. This will save you time sifting through property particulars. Get at least three valuations of your current home from experienced local agents. Remember that as a downsizer you hold a lot of value with estate agents. Chances are you occupy one of the best properties on the market and, once you sell, you'll have cash to spend.

Choose wisely – look for properties that have 'hidden' value: a place where rooms can be repurposed – the garage into an office, the study doubling up as a guest bedroom – or a home that offers the possibility to extend (a loft conversion or portion of land for development).

Bottom line: Small can be beautiful, even if it takes a little getting used to.

7

Rooms for Improvement

'Fashions fade — style is eternal.'

Yves Saint Laurent

1 Cherish your home's true style

All properties come with a timeline, distinctive characteristics specific to their era. Over the years, successive homeowners put their stamp on a place by adding 'fresh' features, but too many fall into the trap of papering over the old to make way for the new and, in so doing, chip away at a property's intrinsic value.

We might not categorise houses from the fifties, 'swinging' sixties or even seventies as period properties, but they're increasingly appreciated for their retro charms, as seen in rising demand and resale values. It's for those reasons that property experts recommend staying true to a home's original design. It's not about waiting for that period to come back into fashion, but rather to maximise a property's potential by giving it the historical context it deserves.

So, if stripping out the fancy tiling in your Victorian conversion or removing the panelling in your sixties semi sounds tempting, temper your instincts and work instead towards making the best of what you have. Do some research at your local library and find out how your home would have looked when it was built. Salvage original features such as balusters, beams and dado rails, and, where possible, repair, rather than replace items. Those that can't be saved, try to at least match the design by sourcing antique or reproduction alternatives. It takes time and effort to coax a place back to life, but you'll be rewarded with the biggest high, knowing you've brought out its true personality.

Bottom line: Stay true to your home's original design – it will add financial as well as aesthetic value.

2 Perfect your extension

'For good plans you pay now. For bad plans you may pay now and will pay later.'

Ralph Pressel (home design expert)

Home extensions vary hugely in price depending on square footage and design specifications. Done well, however, they can add more to a home's value than any other single improvement. The decision to grow 'up' or 'out' will be dictated largely by plot dimensions and boundaries. Many back and side extensions, for example, no longer require planning permission and can be built under 'permitted development rights'.

Building Regulations approval is, however, required for all extensions, no matter how small. Your electrician or builder should be able to obtain approval for minor work such as rewiring, but for larger projects, you'll need the expertise of an architect to draw up project plans for submission to the local council for approval.

The golden rule when working out a budget is to avoid 'over-capitalisation'. Your financial outlay should be directly linked to the value any improvements may generate. For a standard home worth £400,000, it's worth spending in the region of £80,000-£100,000. For mid-range properties, the investment should be proportionally less.

Before you commit any funds, have your property valued. Most neighbourhoods have a 'ceiling price' – buyers won't go above a certain amount no matter how attractive your spanking new granny annexe may be – so check with local agents to avoid pricing your home out of its postcode. It's also worth enquiring whether your extension will nudge you into a higher council tax band; speak to neighbours who have had similar work done and contact your local authority for confirmation.

Pick of the best

Loft conversions – *the* perfect way to create that much-prized extra bedroom, a loft conversion can add as much as 15 per cent to your home's value, provided you get the positioning of the stairs right and can build in extra headroom and light with the addition of dormer windows. Expect to pay upwards of £25,000 for a small conversion, £60,000+ for a grander affair with *en suite* trimmings.

Side extensions – a simple way to acquire extra space without sacrificing the best bit of your garden. Allow £20,000 for a modest add-on, upwards of £100,000 for a top-notch, single-storey construction. Bear in mind that building a first-floor extension over an existing part of the house can be much costlier, as the foundations may need to be reinforced.

Conservatories – these offer extra entertaining and reception space, and, provided they relate well to the existing building, can add as much as five per cent to the value of your home, with costs ranging from £5,000 to upwards of £30,000. Think carefully about your choice of glazing. Performance glass such as Celsius (*www.celciusglass.com*) may cost a little more, but will better regulate temperature changes through the seasons.

Bottom line: The cost of an extension must be proportional to the value of your house.

3 Improve for good

'There's always room for improvement you know – it's the biggest room in the house.'

Louise Heath Leber (businesswoman)

'Improve, don't move' has become something of a new age mantra, but not all 'improvements' reap the expected rewards:

Bling bathrooms and kitchens – extravagant Jacuzzis and super-size wet rooms cost a small fortune to install and may well wow the neighbours, but unless you have a rambling country pile where space (and money) is no object, they're likely to be ripped out by your successors because they're tantamount to dead space. Bespoke kitchens are a further cash sapper; buyers seldom distinguish between a well-designed high-street brand that costs £5,000 and a souped-up alternative that costs £10,000, so unless you're planning to stay put and live the dream, rein in your extravagances.

Open-plan layouts – houses tend to be valued by the number of rooms rather than the square footage, with an extra bedroom adding a disproportionate amount of weight in market value. Trendy open-plan kitchen/diners can be an effective way of combating space limitations, but may limit your buyer base and have a negative impact on the selling price.

Quirky decor – bespoke interiors that indulge the eccentricities of the owner can have prospective buyers running to the hills. Purchasers look for understated quality, not garish gimmicks. So keep the red-hot upholstery and mirrored ceilings to a minimum.

Poor maintenance – prevention is better than cure. So check your chimney, clear your gutters and make sure your wiring is up to scratch. If buyers see DIY projects that need doing the minute they move in, they'll scale back their offer.

Bottom line: Improvements are all well and good, but not at the expense of your property's character, floor space and 'liveability'.

4 Big up your living space

'Focus 90 per cent of your time on solutions and only 10 per cent of your time on problems.'

Anthony J D'Angelo (US author)

Reconfiguring existing living space offers instant payback – it's quick and easy to do, costs next to nothing and doesn't require planning approval. From clever storage and multi-purpose furniture to one-step structural changes, the key is to maximise the usable space in the rooms in which you spend most of your time.

Partitions – knocking down a partition wall is the simplest way to create a more versatile, multi-tasking living area. Open-plan arrangements work best if you highlight key zones such as living, dining and work. You can do this with the help of accent lighting, and a mixed floor surface. Select a colour theme for the entire space and add a couple of signature tones for accent. Stick to just one or two large-scale items of furniture with a common thread that connects the zones together, be it the style, colour or fabric. Leave small pieces out of the equation – they'll just make the area look cluttered.

Storage – built-in storage units that extend to the ceiling are perfect for squirreling away clutter, while modular units offer a versatile back-up for day-to-day use and can be added to suit your changing needs. Shelving is best for books, but if you opt for wider ledges you'll squeeze an extra rows worth in. Alcoves and awkward nooks and crannies make great cupboard space, while the space under the stairs can be kitted out with hooks and racks for miscellaneous knick-knacks.

Decor – for a free-flowing space, visually connect adjoining rooms by using complementary materials on walls and floor surfaces and arrange furniture so that it doesn't block windows or doors. The further you can see through a space, the larger it will seem. Keep your colour palette pale – that way, light reflects off the floors and walls opening up the room. For very tight spaces, think about having vertical radiators installed. They don't need to be worked around and can also be customised to accommodate angles and curves. Dual-purpose furniture now comes in a variety of whacky forms from beds with TVs secreted in their footboards to pullout under-stair study/home offices.

Bottom line: Every house has dormant space – find yours and use it.

5 Get green fingered

'If you want to feel better, get out into a garden.'

Alan Titchmarsh

A well-kept garden is a 'growing' investment and could even be the determining factor in a sale, so if your backyard is a more wild and free 'nature reserve' than Hampton Court offshoot, try the following easy-care tips for a pristine patch:

Keep it simple – garden design these days is a lot more wholesome than it used to be. Vegetables and fruit now shine as the decorative border stars among the flowering shrubs – aping centuries-old cottage garden traditions. So make the backbone of your garden hardy perennials like viburnum, ceanothus and escallonia that take care of themselves. As for the veggies, start with good plants or seeds, give them what they want – food, water and light – and they'll do all the hard work for you.

Think vertically as well as horizontally – use trellising or fences to create a more private space and boost your bloom count. Structures such as pergolas and gazebos can also provide planting opportunities for climbers. For year round interest, use an evergreen favourite such as ivy and intersperse with flowering species such as jasmine, clematis or honeysuckle. Alternatively, create interest at eye level by mounting planters filled with trailing flowers.

Furnish the outdoors – al fresco dining gives you the perfect excuse to revamp your terrace/patio area. Barring a roof, you essentially have all the features of a room to play with including flooring, walls and furniture. Treat walls and fences in the same way as your interior – give them a lick of paint or add texture by covering them with willow, heather or bamboo screening. Keep floors natural – try limestone, granite or high-grade sustainable timber. Always go for the best you can afford with outdoor furniture – wrought iron, teak and cedar are timeless and hard wearing and will keep their lustre for years. As for barbecues – try a fun alternative like a chiminea (cast-iron or clay Mexican oven). They'll keep you warm as the daytime temperature drops and grill your supper in style at the same time.

Bottom line: Think of your garden as the 'happy room' – you not only get a nice green fix, you've also got somewhere special to entertain.

6 Choose your colour scheme wisely

*'All colours are the friends of their neighbours and the
lovers of their opposites.'*

Marc Chagall

Making a poor colour choice can knock hundreds of
pounds off a home's sale price and it's easy to see why.
Colour evokes an intuitive response in us all, which means
that while headstrong vibrant hues may bring out the best
in you, they stand to alienate a high percentage of your
purchaser base.

Magnolia's timeless appeal is in its ability to give a
heightened sense of space, while giving other colours
room to breathe. Its serenity inducing tone, however, can
also absolve us from taking risks. Paint your walls taupe,
'match' it with beige-coloured furniture and fabrics, and
before you know it, you're living in a big bland box.
Neutral colours should, instead, be used as the backdrop,
a way of building up complementary tonal ranges through
furnishings, fabrics and accessories – soft yellows and
golds, mid-browns and caramels that whisper 'well-
considered decoration' not 'party-on central'.

Dos and don'ts

- Always test out colours by buying samples
  and painting a large square of wall, or paint onto
  sections of lining paper and stick them up. Watch

how the colour alters during different times of the day in different light to make sure you still like the shade. Use websites like *www.dulux.co.uk* or *www.crownpaint.co.uk* to play around with colour schemes before stepping into a DIY store.

- Lighter colours don't always make a room look bigger. A small room painted white with a beige carpet and pale furnishings won't appear larger, as neutral shades don't encourage the eye to travel. You'll see the room in one take and you're done. To create a feeling of space, opt instead for a colour from the mid-range tones such as lilac, cool blue or soft green. They're quiet enough to satisfy the need for serenity, but have enough depth to entertain the eye. Remember that colour also appears darker at night, on a small wall or in a room with minimal exposure.

- Always consider the position and outlook of the room: north-facing rooms can feel mournful and uninviting so use warm colours that have the look of fire and sunshine, such as red, magenta and terracotta. Likewise, sunny south-facing rooms will look cool, crisp and fresh with passive pale blues and greens.

- Steer clear of bold colours in rooms that you use frequently and stick to the more gentle side of the spectrum – creams, grey-greens and violets. Oft-neglected entrance halls and stairwells, while important as 'first impression' areas (as well as linking individual rooms) can take a stronger shade because they're transitory space.

- Don't neglect paint finish – like colours, choices can be overwhelming, but if you don't want to be stripping down your handiwork in the months to come, you need to choose a product that's fit for purpose. For ceiling and walls, a water-based matt or silk emulsion works best. If it's a small room, try a light shade with a reflective silky sheen for the illusion of extra space. Matt emulsion is brilliant at masking uneven surfaces and imperfections. Woodwork and trims see plenty of wear and tear, so choose a durable oil-based paint that can be wiped clean.

Bottom line: Unless you like living in a battlefield, go easy on the strong colours.

7 Find interior inspiration

'Nothing is in good taste unless it suits the way you live.'

Billy Baldwin (interior designer)

An interior makeover doesn't have to be a big money production. If all you're after is a few ideas, colour guidance or help arranging furniture, you'll find many design consultants are more than happy to come to your home and give you advice by the hour, leaving you with layout suggestions, colour swatches and sketches. To get the most out of the experience, draw up a draft budget in advance and get together a 'stamp book' of cut-outs from magazines of favourite styles, so your designer has a head start in creating a space specifically for you. Get them to check the feasibility of your budget, and show you how to allocate portions of it to different areas of expense – curtains, furnishing fabrics, light fittings, accessories and designer's fees. This will help you to prioritise your decoration requirements.

An often overlooked alternative can be found on the high street. Shops such as John Lewis, Habitat, and Laura Ashley, as well as online companies like OKA (*www.okadirect.com*) and Dwell (*www.dwell.co.uk*), offer design services that cost next to nothing. They work on the principle that you'll probably buy your makeover essentials from them. Some visit a client's home, come up with mood boards, furniture suggestions and window-dressing plans, then co-ordinate delivery and installation. Others will not just source furniture, but will project manage a revamp, from flooring and fixing blinds to putting the last mug on the rack.

Bottom line: An interior designer can filter your needs, wants and fantasies through their professional sensibility, so try one for size.

8 Experiment with scale

'Always scale up, not down. Everyone is terrified of making things too big. If in doubt, make it bigger, not smaller.'

Roger Banks Pye (interior designer)

Many home-makers side-step the 'technical' planning stage when decorating and furnishing a home, as it seems a bit too much like hard work. But testing your ideas on a scale model can save a lot of time and aggro. It allows you to input dimensions and furniture sizes to make an exact scale of your room without lugging heavy sofas and tables around for an hour. The easiest way to draw a plan is with the help of simple interior software packages such as Arcon 3D Architect and Ideal Home 3D Home Design or online space-planning tools like *www.spaceplanning.com* and *www.mydeco.com*. Your designs and layouts can be created, saved, modified and shared with others by e-mail. No specialist computer skills are required, beyond the ability to point and click with your mouse. Two-dimensional drawing plans consisting of walls, doors, windows and other icons represent anything from furniture to stereo equipment. Once these are slotted into the plan, they can then be easily manipulated to change size and location.

Remember to build plenty of circulation space into your plan. As a rule of thumb, 2 ft is a workable minimum to allow per person to move about freely. Always allow extra space for opening doors and drawers. If your beloved ottoman sofa is too big 'on-plan', try it elsewhere in the room and be prepared to change it for a more streamlined version if necessary.

Bottom line: Scale is all-important when designing, so mind your proportions.

8

Abodes Abroad

1 Remove the rose-tinted spectacles

'If you want a place in the sun, you've got to put up with a few blisters.'

Abigail Van Buren (US advice columnist)

Lots of second-homers feel guilty for not spending enough 'quality time' at their property. Others jet off for their annual 'fun in the sun fix', while secretly hankering for a change. If you're the kind of person who thrives on spontaneity and five-star fluffy bathrobe luxury, chances are a second home will simply leave you feeling like a disgruntled extra in *Groundhog Day*. Peripatetic types can always opt for the pack-and-go delights of a motor home. But fixed abode second-homers whose budget doesn't stretch to the luxury of hired help are likely to feel hard done by, faced with an annual sentence of cooking, cleaning and property maintenance.

A lifetime of *Waltons*-style family holidays may also sound idyllic, but in reality few properties offer the degree of flexibility likely to sustain your long-term needs and interests. That middle of nowhere rural retreat that's perfect for loved up couples might be too isolated for toddlers or simply 'down right boring' for teenagers. Similarly, your younger kids might be in their element in a lively beachfront location, but you may find it too crowded once you've retired. In fact, the very attributes that draw you to a location may turn out to be its biggest turn-offs. So before you commit, think about the alternatives – it could be that renting a piece of paradise turns out to be far more rewarding than buying it outright.

Bottom line: A second home isn't everyone's dream come true.

2 Give your property the twice over

'Great things are not done by impulse, but by a series of small things brought together.'

Vincent Van Gogh

Impulse purchases rarely make sound investments; so if you have a pleasant tingling in your bones about a place, put it to the test. That beachfront villa may look irresistible when the sun's out, but will it be quite as alluring in the depths of winter? In many countries the winter months mean a dramatic change in accessibility (flights, train schedules), climate (leaden skies or tropical storms) and available amenities (many businesses and facilities shut down during the quieter months). So make a point of visiting the region *at least* twice, once in the high season and also during the off-peak months.

Whirlwind inspection trips organised by developers or agents can be a good introduction to an area (you might even get a free stay out of it), but wine-dine-and-sign-on-the-line tours should only ever be for testing the investment waters. For subsequent visits, set your own agenda. Get a feel for what makes the region tick and what attractions will keep you coming back for more.

Visit places you like again without a sales chaperone chattering in your ear; better still, drop in without an appointment to see what's really going on behind the scenes. Take time, too, to view a range of other properties with local agents and compare neighbourhoods and price points. Before you leave, get an 'insider view' from UK owners with property to let in the region – you can follow this up back home through rental websites such as *www.holiday-rentals.co.uk*. Having a good nose around is essential before buying any property. If your love-at-first-sight purchase is meant to be, due diligence won't stand in your way.

Bottom line: The happiest second-homers are clued up about what they're getting into – so root out the reality behind the dream.

3 Check the price is right

'Knowledge is of no value unless you put it into practice.'

Heber J. Grant (Mormon apostle)

Assessing a property's true market value is rarely a simple tick-box process. The asking price may *seem* reasonable, based on Western perceptions, but only by checking out the competition will you know if it's a fair deal. An essential first step is to ascertain whether the property has been quoted to you in 'local' or 'foreign' pricing. Many countries maintain a 'two-tier' system and for good reason. With new-build property UK agents earn hefty commissions for marketing overseas projects, with those fees recouped in price mark-ups. But you won't know about it until you start speaking to trusted *local* agents, visiting properties and seeing what else is on offer. A further 'hidden' profit margin unlikely to be flagged up in the sales pitch is the resort fee. Often listed as administration or transaction costs, this charge is over and above basic annual operating expenses. If the figure seems artificially high compared to other resorts, challenge the developer.

Dual pricing isn't only applicable to new homes. In popular tourist spots, it's not unusual for a resale property to have a built-in premium calibrated towards 'wealthy' second home buyers. This happens because there's an assumption that foreigners will typically pay more because it's cheaper than a similar property at home, but also because many people have unrealistic expectations about their property's value. In some instances estate agents will apportion fees to both buyer and seller, effectively doubling their commission. So keep your eyes and ears open and don't be afraid to negotiate if the numbers seem high. Ignorance is no excuse for paying over the odds.

Bottom line: If the price isn't right – walk away.

4 Do the six-point diligence drill

'Ignorance is not bliss. It's fatal. You either get organised or get crushed.'

Donald Trump

There's something quaintly reassuring about the Herculean mound of paperwork that comes with buying property at home, from Land Registry checks and structural surveys to sorting finance and buildings insurance. Why some buyers throw caution to the wind when buying thousands of miles away therefore remains a mystery. In fact, making a buy-wise purchase in foreign climes isn't as complex as it may first appear, provided you stick to a few basic rules:

Look at the bigger picture – research macro factors such as a country's political and economic situation. Investigate tourism statistics, stability of currency, as well as property growth trends and the government's stance on foreign ownership. Go to *www.fco.gov.uk* and *www.fopdac.com* for up-to-date location profiles.

Sort your finances – if you're arranging finance on a property, ensure that this is clearly stated in any contract. Where possible, seek an 'opt-out' clause if the loan is not agreed. This will ensure any deposit paid is refunded.

Know your legal rights – some emerging markets offer limited protection to overseas buyers, so find out what restrictions are put on foreign property holders, including the maximum length of stay, visa requirements and what appropriation rights the government holds in the region. Where do you stand if the developer or vendor fails to deliver on what they've promised? What is the dispute resolution process?

Appoint an independent solicitor – choose someone located in the country you're buying who can represent you throughout your purchase. They shouldn't have anything to do with the property or the developer and *must* be proficient in property transactions with foreigners. The Law Society and the British Consulate can supply names of country-specific solicitors.

Check the title deeds – it's essential to verify that the home you're purchasing has clean title, for instance, that ownership is undisputed, boundaries are clearly delineated and that you won't inherit any debt. Check the planning status of new-build property. Does the developer have full title to the land or property? If the property has been built in the last 20 years you should insist on seeing evidence that it has the correct planning consent. If you're intending to carry out restoration or extension work on an older property, now is also the time to check that this is allowable and to apply for permission.

Tackle the tax system – find out if your country of purchase has a tax treaty with the UK to ensure you're not taxed twice on any income. The UK, for example, has a double taxation treaty with France and Italy, but still doesn't have one with Costa Rica. Some places have a 'two-tier' tax system where rates paid by locals are substantially less than those paid by foreigners; so make sure you're analysing the cash flow based on the latter. It's also important to find out your inheritance and capital gains tax liabilities for when you come to sell. Inheritance laws are often far less flexible than in the UK, so if you live or hold substantial assets abroad, it's worth having a local will drawn up.

Bottom line: Buying abroad isn't the time for a due diligence bypass.

5 Make your bolt-hole pay its way

'No man acquires property without acquiring with it a little arithmetic also.'

Ralph Waldo Emerson (US poet/philosopher)

If you're only spending a few weeks a year at your property, it makes sense to get some rental mileage out of it, to help pay towards its upkeep. Certain countries impose restrictions on short-term lets to protect their own full-time residents – the States is a case in point. Likewise, in Spain you need to register and seek permission from the local authority if you want to rent your home.

Rental income generated on a second home abroad is subject to UK income tax based on your marginal rate. You can, however, claim for certain expenses and thereby reduce your tax liability. Typically, these will include repairs, utility bills, rates, insurance and letting administration costs. If you have a second home mortgage, you can also claim relief against the interest paid on the loan.

Top tips to maximise rentals

Build a profile on the Internet – go for high-volume sites such as *www.holiday-rentals.co.uk*, *www.holidaylettings. co.uk* and *www.ownersdirect.co.uk*; study well-written adverts and do the same. Take good quality photos and upload these onto any online profiles. Creating your own website can also boost your online exposure, but if you use the services of a web designer, just make sure you know how to edit the site yourself.

Start your marketing early – people book their holidays as far as a year in advance (especially ski chalets), so prioritise getting the high-value weeks reserved and be prepared to do deals; it's a great way of building your repeat customer base.

Spread the word – get listed with the local tourist board and leave a stash of flyers at your local tourist information office.

'Seasonalise' your pitch – savvy rentals are all about embracing the seasons. Those with ski chalets should switch their marketing focus in the summer months to attract outdoor lovers – so big up the mountain biking and hiking. Xmas and New Year is the perfect time to showcase the winter wonderland delights on offer with snow-clad photos and cosy log fire close-ups. Short breaks geared towards retirees or those with preschool kids are ideal to slot into the shoulder season (the period that falls between high and low season).

Listen to client feedback – if they suggest putting a portable TV in the bedroom, then do it. In a tough market, tuning into your target audience can make the difference between a same-time-next-year booking and losing out to your competitors.

Bottom line: Think about your target market and fine tune your marketing efforts accordingly.

6 Get clued up on currencies

'The safe way to double your money is to fold it over once and put it in your pocket.'

Frank McKinney Hubbard (humourist)

Fluctuations in the exchange rate can significantly affect the sterling price of your overseas home, which makes finding the best exchange rate and methods of transfer a top priority. Many buyers avoid playing currency roulette by either tapping into existing savings or taking out a second mortgage on their UK residence. This is by far the cheapest and easiest way if you have equity in your current home, as long as you bear in mind currency conversion costs. Remember, large deposits (on average 10 per cent of the property value) are required on foreign property purchases.

Those changing pounds to foreign currency have two main options open to them: teaming up with either a high-street bank or a foreign exchange specialist such as *www.currenciesdirect.com* or *www.caxtonfx.com*. Specialist brokers invariably offer a better deal: more competitive rates, lower (if any) transfer fees and no commission charges. Because they solely deal in foreign exchange, you'll also benefit from a number of exchange perks that most banks are unable to offer:

Spot contract – this involves the buying of currency there and then at an agreed rate usually for immediate delivery and can be beneficial if, for example, the rates offered by your broker are low when buying a certain amount of foreign currency. Minimum buying amount is usually between £2,000 and £5,000.

Forward contract – a forward contract is effectively a 'buy now pay later' scheme, allowing you to 'lock into' a favourable rate for up to two years. The added benefit of this type of contract is flexibility – you can draw down some or all of your currency up to three months prior to the forward date that you've set in place, which is particularly useful if your completion date is pushed back.

Regular payment plan – this works best for those who have regular payments to make in a country such as a pension or mortgage payments. A direct debit payment is normally set up with a minimum monthly transaction of £150 and the flexibility to up the amount as and when needed. Again, short-term competitive exchange rates can be fixed.

Orders – these are ideally suited to buyers who are not in a rush to transfer money or to buy currency, and who can wait for an optimum rate to save money. Stop loss orders enable you to fix a minimum rate at which the currency is bought or sold. If the exchange rate drops below this level, you are not affected. Limit orders, on the other hand, allow you to set an optimum exchange rate, which, if achieved, enables you to purchase your currency.

Choosing the right company can be made easier by drawing up a basic check-list taking into account service levels, country-specific expertise and best combination of rates. It's also wise to request a personally assigned dealer.

If there's a rate that you desire, your broker will ensure that the rate is 'booked' when it's achieved. Brokers' abilities to access 'live' exchange rates means that they should be able to undercut banks, which work to built-in margins. That said, if you're a long-standing customer with one of the major high-street names, you've nothing to lose by putting in a call to see what's on offer.

Bottom line: Buying abroad is costly enough without losing out on currency fluctuations – so seek specialist advice.

7 Take guaranteed returns with a pinch of salt

'If you want a guarantee, buy a toaster.'

Clint Eastwood

Developers have a raft of sweeteners up their sleeves to woo buyers to their yet-to-be-built properties. A firm favourite is guaranteed rental returns (GRR). At face value, quoted yields of five to seven per cent per annum for a three-year period look tempting. Many projects, however, will be operating behind a smoke screen of empty promises rather than cold, hard cash. Some developers finance their GRR offer by striking deals with tour operators to take a quota of apartments for a fixed period. Others will simply add a sneaky five per cent to the asking price and return the money to the buyer in the form of 'guaranteed' rent. Even if the property never sees a single rental, it won't have cost the developer a penny.

It's also important to think ahead to when the 'guaranteed period' ends. By that stage, your property will be up against a raft of newer, shinier alternatives. If competition is stiff, the pressure on rentals and market values of the units could go down rather than up. If it's an up-and-coming area, you may even find yourself struggling to find tenants at all. In cases where a regular rental income is a priority, a more reliable option is to buy where you have hotel branding and management, as the relevant chain will work hard to bring the clients in. Bear in mind, however, that your own use of the property (under the terms of the contract) will come with restrictions, such as limited access during peak season.

As with any investment, the guarantee you get is only as strong as the company that underwrites it, so even if the GRR seems reasonable, you need to be sure that the developer or resort operator has the financial wherewithal to sustain the returns if the rental or sales market takes a turn for the worse. In many cases, the contract also gives the developer the right to terminate the GRR agreement by giving several months' notice – so check the small print before you sign.

Bottom line: GRR means nothing without an established rentals market – make sure yields quoted are based on actual figures.

8 Old or new – decide what works for you

'You are never too old to set another goal or to dream a new dream.'

C S Lewis

Age-mellowed countries like France and Italy are chock-a-block with traditional property, drawing buyers who value character over and above novelty. Opting for an older house can certainly be a savvy investment if you're 'in it' for the long term. Supply is limited. Locations are invariably top-notch, plus you can wallow in bricks and mortar authenticity. More mature abodes, however, can be a drain on your finances and precious spare time; if major repairs are required, you'll either have to roll up your sleeves and do it yourself or call in the professionals. This is all well and good if you can rise above the long-distance hassles and the monthly bills. If not, you might be better off culling your period fantasy and settling for a younger, lower-maintenance model.

New-build has its share of upsides, from quality construction and contemporary styling to energy-efficient heating and air-conditioning plus all the latest mod con goodies. If the resort or neighbourhood you're buying into is amenity laden, you'll also hold a competitive advantage over stand-alone equivalents that lack these benefits. But shiny and new isn't without its negatives. Price per square foot invariably works out more expensive than a resale home of a similar size. Property choice and on-site amenities can also vary hugely with location; so individual set-ups need to be looked at with a critical eye. Is the pool big enough to accommodate multiple well-endowed families? What about property plot sizes and annual maintenance costs? Don't forget to factor in intangibles to the decision-making process too. Similarly styled homes tend, for example, to attract like-minded buyers, with most developments geared towards 'fun-loving' families. Depending on your point of view, however, a daily diet of cookie-cutter conformity, not to mention other people's kids might end up being more of a curse than a blessing.

Bottom line: Apply logic, not emotion, when buying abroad.

9 Plan your exit strategy

'The time to prepare isn't after you have been given the opportunity. It's long before that opportunity arises.'

John Wooden (US basketball coach/writer)

It seems strange to think about the end game when purchasing a holiday home, but savvy buyers always plan their escape route, their 'back door'. They size up their target audience and work with a realistic 'sell-on' time frame in mind. To get a feel for how buoyant your local resale market is, count the number of distinct buyer groups. If you've three or more, including local, national and overseas, you've got a healthy base to work from. If one or more of these investor pools dries up, you'll still have plenty of 'potentials' left in reserve. Most selling-up problems tend to occur where a location is overly reliant on one single investment stream. Certain Caribbean islands, where tourism has historically been dependent on US and UK markets, fall into this category. If that particular market softens, property investors can be left exposed, especially if the local population has been priced out of the market and can't afford to buy in.

To ensure a well-conceived exit strategy, make sure what you buy has the edge over its competition. Choose a prime location with protected natural or historical assets where development is restricted, a rural spot perhaps that's benefiting from reverse migration, where locals are moving back for a better quality of life. Look to an area's future, too, before committing to any purchase. Transport access, tour operator presence and rental zone changes can all dramatically affect the resale value of a property, taking an area from boom to bust or vice versa, so research historical price trends (from the Land Registry or national statistics offices) and pinpoint where buyer demand will come from. Think of it as working in reverse – then you can enjoy the journey.

Bottom line: 'Future-proof' your property purchase – start with the end in mind.

9

Successful Selling

1 Be prepared

> *'Success always comes when preparation meets opportunity.'*
>
> Henry Hartman (artist and illustrator)

Nobody wants to fall victim to unrealistic property valuations, something that can easily be avoided by doing some basic background research to compare local prices and how the market is performing, *before* you speak to any agents. For accurate data, check out the Land Registry's free price analysis search service (*www.landregistry.gov.uk*). By finding property in your area comparable to yours that has sold within the last few months, you can gauge what your own home is likely to fetch. Armed with this knowledge, you can then solicit valuations from two or three local agents. When you do, keep your findings to yourself and don't discuss competitors' findings – it will only colour their valuation.

Take time as well to assess the true condition of your

property. Work that needs doing can be carried out or disclosed ahead of sale, minimising the risk of a buyer price 'chip' in response to foreseeable problems. Either commission a presale survey from a chartered surveyor, which will set you back between £500 and £1,500, or, if budgets are tight, ask a couple of local builders to give your home the once over. Most will do it for free if they think there's a job in the pipeline. All this may seem like overkill, but compared to a lost sale, it's time and effort well spent.

Bottom line: Understand the game before you roll the dice.

2 Keep the TLC low-key

'If you do the little jobs well, the big ones tend to take care of themselves.'

Dale Carnegie

Showing your home to its best advantage is an essential part of any successful sales strategy, but frittering away time and money on last minute renovations can end up doing more harm than good. Today's volatile housing market is making valuers reconsider previously held assumptions of what home improvements *actually* add in terms of value. Instead of advocating a top-to-toe overhaul, most agree you can improve a property's saleability by simply tending to the DIY basics such as chipped paintwork and leaking taps, de-cluttering and applying some good old-fashioned elbow grease.

So if your home is more down-and-out than show home chic – just leave it. Renovation 'projects' will always appeal to a certain type of buyer. By shelling out a fortune to make your home look immaculate, people will sense that they're paying a premium and retreat to something more 'on their level'.

By the same token, a dowdy house in reasonable condition will benefit from a lick of paint, but shelve the major makeover plans. Most buyers prioritise space above improvement potential. But that doesn't have to mean 'extra square footage' in the form of an extension. Being creative with the space you already have is the quickest, cheapest route to adding value – think dual-purpose study/spare bedroom or extra storage space in the loft. If your apartment is in competition with an identical flat that boasts ceiling-to-floor storage, that's the one likely to get snapped up first. As tempting as it may be to spend your way to home perfection, think first about how you can spruce up what you have.

Bottom line: Shelve the grand design schemes and make good with some TLC instead.

3 Get on good terms with your agent

'Start with what is right rather than what is acceptable.'

Franz Kafka

Agency fees are based on three principal criteria: prevailing market conditions, the number of competitor agents on 'their patch' and geographical location. Buyers who secure the best fees do so by wily negotiation. So start by visiting the main agents in your area, short-list three and enquire about their fee structures. If a particular firm appeals, let them think that it's between them and another firm, but that their fee isn't as 'competitive'. The ball is now in their court to win your business with a better offer. Sole agents will typically quote you two to two and a half per cent +VAT; your goal should be to get them down to one to one and a half per cent +VAT. For property over £500,000 you should aim to go even lower.

Lengthy lock-in periods can be a further stumbling block. Considerable time, effort and expense goes behind successfully marketing a property, so it's not unreasonable for an agent to request a decent time period to show 'what they're made of', but an initial four to six week tenure is ample. By keeping the trial period short and sweet, you'll not only maximise an agent's effort during the 'new instruction' phase, you can also pull the plug and go elsewhere if they're not coming up with the goods. Be mindful, too, of timing when it comes to fees. A favourite ruse by agents is to try and secure payment on exchange. If a contract is vague about this, don't sign. A sale can still fall through between exchange and completion, so be sure you only pay fees *after* the deal has been completed.

Bottom line: There's always room for negotiation, whatever you're told.

4 Gazunder-proof your sale

It's the phone call that sellers dread – just days from exchanging contracts the buyer rings to ask for a price reduction or 'they'll walk'. As rife at the first-time buyer end of the market as it is higher up the food chain, 'gazundering' puts the seller in the impossible position of having to 'agree' to the lower price or face putting their place back on the market and risk losing the dream house they were about to buy. Seasoned gazunderers work on the principle that most sellers will take the lower offer just to keep the show on the road. The softer the market, the more likely buyers are to chance their luck. So what steps can you take to avoid being held to ransom?

Top tips

Pre-qualify your buyers – chain-free buyers with mortgage offers in place move quicker than those without; speed reduces the likelihood of anyone claiming that the value of your home has fallen since the original offer was made, so keep time frames for completion tight – six to eight weeks is more than reasonable.

Launch a pre-emptive strike – issues often crop up during surveys, which can lead to a price adjustment. Nip this in the bud by assessing your home's condition before you market it; you can then discuss any problems from a position of knowledge and insight and weed out bogus claims. If you do find defects, flag them up with the buyer.

That way, it will be far harder for them to haggle down the price at the last minute.

Keep your distance – avoid direct renegotiations with the buyer. If the reduced offer comes straight from the purchaser, go back to your agent and seek their advice – they're much better equipped to handle the situation because they're not personally or emotionally involved.

Have a back-up plan – remember, you're not home and dry until contracts have been exchanged, so keep your property on the market until then. If problems do arise, you've still got other potential buyers in the frame.

Bottom line: Gazundering is nothing short of blackmail – don't give in to it.

5 Work on the chain gang

'A chain is only as strong as its weakest link.'

Proverb

They say that moving house is one of life's most stressful events, but being stuck in an immovable chain comes a close second. Hold-ups occur for any number of reasons: incomplete paperwork, difficulties securing a loan, or a buyer pulling out on the strength of a survey. Steps, however, can be taken to avoid snarl-ups and stop a sale unravelling.

Top tips

Vet the contestants – serious buyers will have someone lined up to purchase their place, a mortgage offer agreed in principle and a solicitor waiting in the wings; so sound them out with a few politely detailed questions. If a buyer is coy about their personal or financial circumstances, get your agent to probe further.

Serve a notice to complete – if you've exchanged contracts but your buyer is dithering, a notice will set a deadline for the other side to have everything signed off within ten days. Failure to do so means they run the risk of losing their deposit.

Break the chain – the fewer parties there are in the chain, the less likely it is for the deal to flounder, so consider moving into temporary accommodation or even renting. A short-term let could actually save you cash – the increased buying power you get often more than offsets the cost of renting.

Drop the price – if the sticking point is money, speak to your agent and see whether you can reach a compromise by accepting a little less for your property by negotiating down the chain. If everyone drops their price by five per cent, it can hold the deal together.

Bottom line: A chain is only as strong as its weakest link – the more links, the higher your risk.

6 Showcase your place

'Sex appeal is fifty per cent what you've got and fifty per cent what people think you've got.'

Sophia Loren

Getting your home ready for viewing is like preparing a set for a blockbuster movie – you need to get the atmosphere, props and lighting right before the cameras start rolling. Why? Because your buyer audience will decide within minutes of viewing whether or not your property is a hit: an unkempt garden or peeling paintwork is often all it takes to secure a lousy review. Giving your house kerb appeal, however, isn't just about dressing for effect. It's about encouraging potential buyers to make an emotional connection, to see how easy it will be to live there, rather than spend time imagining how the place might look and how hard it might be to whip it into shape. So how do you go about showing your home to best effect?

Get snap happy – it's human nature to overlook what we see every day, but when you see things on screen, you get a much needed 'other view'. So take photographs of your property and look at them on the computer. It will allow you to critique each room in sequence and make improvements accordingly.

Lose the 'me, myself, I' – your home is no longer yours once that 'for sale' sign goes up, but you still need to prepare it so potential new owners pick up on the positive undercurrents of your efforts. Start by depersonalising and neutralising spaces: remove photos, clothing and personal items and replace them with more generic alternatives. You can still give your home personality with carefully chosen items such as decorative mirrors or scatter cushions; just keep the family heirlooms and kiddie art to a minimum.

Make an entrance – the exterior of your home is the first thing potential buyers see. So take a look at your property from across the road; make sure your front garden frames the house with a design that gives it character, but which also complements the street. Keep garden paths wide and weed-free to emphasise the feeling of arrival and separate any driveway with small trees and hedging plants. Give your front door a fresh coat of paint and stick with quality door furniture that suits the age and style of the property.

Conquer clutter – an excess of clobber makes it difficult to concentrate on what you're viewing; the more we see in a room, the less we process. Clutter also has the knack for making everything look smaller, so strip back rooms. Put large items of furniture, knick-knacks and books into storage. Prune furniture: people tend to line their walls with chairs and tables, but 'floating' furniture away from walls into cosy groups makes the traffic flow more obvious and the perimeters clear.

Light the way – atmosphere is best created by varying light levels according to your mood and the time of day, so install dimmers. Remedy bad lighting by increasing the wattage in your lamps and fittings. Aim for a combination of floor, table and overhead lighting in key rooms to create contrast and highlight eye-catching objects.

Bottom line: Selling your home 'as is' helps sell the competition, so put time and effort into making a good first impression.

7 Make a saving online

'Cut out the middleman. Find someone you hate and buy them a house.'

Kenny Smyth (Australian TV series character)

Selling your home online is a viable, value-for-money alternative to signing with a high-street agent and can save you thousands of pounds in fees. Buyers keen to surf their way to a sale have two main options open to them: teaming up with an online agent or advertising on private property sales websites.

Private property sales (PPS) websites such as *www.home.co.uk* and *www.mypropertyforsale.co.uk* are the equivalent of the classified ads section in the newspaper – except you reach a much wider audience. A one-off charge of around £50 will buy you a basic advert with photo and particulars on that site; a higher fee of £299 + VAT will secure you broader exposure on some, *but not all* of the top property listing sites such as *www.propertyfinder.com* and *www.zoopla.co.uk*. Bear in mind, however, that PPS websites only *advertise* your property and field initial enquiries. The rest, including conducting viewings and negotiating with potential buyers, is down to you.

Top tips

Check the small print – many sellers choose to 'beef up' their sale prospects by registering with a private sale website as well as using the services of an agent. If you decide to run with both, make sure that your agent hasn't slipped an 'exclusion of private Internet advertising' clause into the contract. If they have, you may still be liable to pay the agency fee, even if you secure a sale through the website. Don't be shy about asking for the term to be removed; if they quibble, take your business elsewhere.

Online estate agents – these are effectively stripped back estate agencies subject to the same rules governing high-street agents. Most, including the biggest – *www.halfapercent.com* and *www.housenetwork.co.uk* – are also members of the National Association of Estate Agents (NAEA) and the Estate Agency Ombudsman scheme. The key benefit of choosing an online agent is the cut-price fee structure. While traditional high-street firms charge between one per cent and three per cent plus VAT for their services, you'll pay around half a per cent to three quarters of a per cent for an online equivalent. The company will arrange all viewings on your behalf, provide particulars to prospective buyers as well as producing a marketing pack (including photos) after visiting your home. What they won't do are the viewings, which will be down to you. As with high-street firms, 'sole agency' rules still apply. This means that if you decide to use both an online *and* a high street agent, you'll need to go 'multiple agency' and pay both parties regardless of who finds the buyer.

Added value – sign up with an online agency and your details will be automatically posted on the main listings portals including the UK's top real estate website *www.rightmove.co.uk*, which doesn't take private adverts from homeowners.

Bottom line: Maximum exposure generates maximum leads – so get your home advertised online.

8 Choose quality over quantity

'The minute you settle for less than you deserve, you get even less than you settled for.'

Maureen Dowd (US columnist)

It's tempting to go with the purchaser who offers the most – but unless they're a cash buyer with a wallet full of readies, accepting the highest offer isn't always in your best interests. Finding a buyer that has been pre-approved for a mortgage and happy to work within your time frame is equally important, so before you agree to any deal, size up your intended and see where they sit on the 'worthy of sale' scale.

Buyer types

First-timers – keenness won't be an issue, but lack of experience might hamper an otherwise glitch-free conveyancing process. To avoid a bumpy ride, sweet-talk your agent into doing a little hand-holding to ensure contractual obligations and deadlines are met.

Contingency buyers – purchasers with a place to shift may not have any firm purchase offers of their own to negotiate on. This means that you're in effect taking responsibility for the sale of two properties. Find out how proactive they're being in marketing their own place; their plan (or lack) of action will speak volumes about their reliability.

In-betweeners – prospective buyers currently renting get Brownie points for being 'chain-free'. Many, however, will be looking to trade up to a bigger property at a discount, which means they'll be angling to buy at the bottom of the market. Accepting a lower offer from a chain-free buyer can work in your favour – *if* you're keen to move quickly. Just be sure your reason for selling outweighs your need to get the best price.

Money-minded investors – those buying purely for financial gain will only have eyes for figures, with rental yields and capital appreciation top of the priority list. Arm yourself with comparative stats and figures of property in your area. Draw their attention to value-added location assets including transport links and local amenities. If your property stacks up, expect a below market value offer for openers and be prepared to haggle.

Bottom line: There's always a trade-off between speed and certainty of sale and price – so pick a buyer that best suits your needs.

10

Gurus to Go

Keep sight of the basics

'Successful property buying doesn't come by second guessing the market, but in getting the fundamentals right. If you do that, and the market drops by 20 per cent, you'll be fine – the house that you bought for a good price, in a good location, may drop in value, but if you bide your time, it will go up eventually. Market logic dictates that in the long term, prices will rise, because people want houses.'

Annie Hulley (property entrepreneur and author of *How to Be a Property Millionaire*)

Suss out the seller

'Loads of property "experts" bang on about adding value, but the truth is there's a limit to how much actual value you can actually add to a property with a refurbishment. And because you can never know with certainty what

will happen to your investment, or the market, in the time it takes you to get your property back in estate agents' windows, it's imperative that you build your best chance of making a profit by buying below the market in the first place. The way to swing things in your favour is to find someone who needs to sell more than you need to buy. If you can find a motivated seller, you can usually find a bargain…'

Gary McCausland (property developer and presenter of Five's *How to be a Property Developer*)

Get to grips with clutter

'We've all got our clutter weaknesses – for some it's clothing, for others paperwork. Recognise them and resolve to get on top of them. Sort through different categories of possessions at regular intervals (weekly, monthly, seasonally or yearly)… Once you have got rid of redundant items and restored order to your home, the benefits will be immediately apparent in an increased sense of space and a more relaxed and productive atmosphere, not to mention in your own satisfaction.'

Sir Terence Conran (designer)

Employ an architect

'Employ an architect and a good one at that, who shares

your view of the world. Don't try and design your home yourself, it's not what you were trained to do. I've had all sorts of design training and I would still employ an architect. A good architect will give you back your dream fully wrought and magnificently detailed – providing you choose the right one.'

Kevin McCloud (presenter of Channel 4's *Grand Designs*)

Find a focus

'Star pieces act as the visual centre of a room, the place to which the eye is drawn. The star piece might be an item of furniture, a piece of artwork, a large mirror or a sculptural light fitting. They demand attention. Luxury is a word, which also needs redefining. Forget gold taps, acres of marble and wall-to-wall glitz. The quest is to find individual things – one-off pieces guarantee originality in a way that luxury brands cannot.'

Kelly Hoppen (interior designer)

Turn detective

'Learn all you can about the vendor's situation and motivation for selling. Successful negotiation is a game that begins much earlier than many think. Ask questions

of everybody involved: what does the agent say the reason for the sale is? Ideally, you should meet Mr and Mrs Vendor separately and ask them both about their situation, reasons for moving, forward plans, marketing history and ideal timescale. If you're viewing with your own partner, split up and speak to them individually. Chat to other local agents who may have viewed the property but failed to get the instruction. They may be able to tell you the true story. If anyone is bluffing, it is sure to come out if you ask enough questions enough times of enough different people.'

Phil Spencer (property expert and co-presenter of Channel 4's *Location, Location, Location*)

Take a step back

'You don't want to walk into a room and feel like your head might explode because there's too much going on. A successful room needs to have balance – too much of one colour, pattern or texture can look busy. Not what you want from your main living space – so do a floor plan before you start so you can see clearly where windows, lighting and furniture are positioned. You can then decide which fabrics to put where. Remember less is more.'

Nina Campbell (interior designer)

Streamline your budget

'If you're going to make any money on renovations, you need to come up with a realistic budget and stick to it. It is up to you to itemise the work you want to do and price up the job realistically. Before you put in an offer, get an idea from a builder as to what your planned renovations might cost (don't forget to add a contingency fund of 20 per cent). When you get the survey through, take note of what it says needs to be done, get a costing on how much any extra work will cost (even though you will have spent money at this point on solicitors and search fees, you can still pull out if the survey has too many unpleasant surprises) and build this into your budget.'

Sarah Beeny (property guru and presenter of Channel 4's *Property Ladder*)

Be a maverick

'I've always worked with the ethos that you should observe the masses and do the opposite, as that's where the opportunities lie. Property investment has always been about a herd mentality – one bank lends, so they all lend. One stops, they all stop. It's an extremist environment, but it doesn't mean either is right or wrong.'

James Caan (business entrepreneur and 'investment angel' on BBC's *Dragons' Den*)

157